With lots of Love,

Maura

xxxx

1st JUNE, 87.

LIFE LESSONS

Volume Two

Witness Lee

Living Stream Ministry
Anaheim, California

First Edition, 6,750 copies. May 1987.

ISBN 0-87083-275-1
(Complete set, softcover)
ISBN 0-87083-277-8
(Lessons 13-24, softcover)

Published by

Living Stream Ministry
1853 W. Ball Road, P. O. Box 2121
Anaheim, CA 92804 U.S.A.

Printed in the United States of America

CONTENTS

EXPLANATION AND FELLOWSHIP

1. These lessons have been specifically prepared for the home meetings of new believers. The first two volumes cover different matters between a believer and God which he should know, understand, and practice immediately after his salvation. Then the last two volumes cover the full salvation which God has prepared in Christ for us who have believed into Him, the riches which we have obtained in Christ, the experience which we should have in Christ, the things which we should accomplish in Christ, and the goal which we should attain in Christ.

2. It is difficult to avoid certain terms which are relatively deep and hard for new believers to understand. There is no need for added explanation while reading these lessons in the meetings. As lesson after lesson is read, a thorough understanding of the terms will be acquired. Even if there is not such a thorough understanding at the time, this understanding will be gained gradually.

3. Knowledge is empty and the letter kills; only Christ is reality and only the Spirit gives life. Thus, there must be prayer, confession of sins, and the abundantly rich filling and saturation with the Spirit of Christ before reading these lessons. In reading, there should be the practice of depending less on the mind and more on the spirit, rejecting the old way of knowledge and emphasizing the new way of life. Sentence after sentence that is being read should be pushed out by the spirit with life that others' spirits may be touched for them to receive the life supply of the pneumatic Christ.

4. The Bible verses in these lessons are quoted in an economical and suitable way. Furthermore, their explanations are both concise and adequate, having no need for further explanation. The only need is to repeat what is read, to emphasize what is read, to read in a living

way, and to pray-read. At times, the reading should be supplemented by hymns or testimonies. Never extend the meaning of the text or develop an understanding based on inference.

5. The Scriptures quoted in these lessons are from the Recovery Version of the New Testament and the King James Version of the Old Testament.

6. For these lessons to be beneficial to the home meetings, there is a great need for much prayer. May the Lord bless His recovery, perfect His saints, and build up His Body.

The author

Taipei
March 20, 1987

KNOWING THE SECTS

The five great items mentioned in the previous six lessons are positive items which we should know; they are the most fundamental truths—realities—revealed by the Bible. Because of the decline and desolation of the church, however, we must also know a most basic negative item in the church's desolation. This is the matter of divisions, the so-called sects or denominations, which we see in Christianity today.

I. HAS CHRIST BEEN DIVIDED?

1) "But I beseech you, brothers, through the name of our Lord Jesus Christ, that you all speak the same thing, and that there be no divisions among you... each of you says, I am of Paul, and I of Apollos, and I of Cephas, and I of Christ. Has Christ been divided? Was Paul crucified for you? Or were you baptized into the name of Paul?" (1 Cor. 1:10-13).

In those days, in the church in Corinth, there were factions. One party said that they were of Paul, and another said that they were of Apollos. Another party said that they were of Cephas (Peter), and still another party, who considered themselves superior to all the previous parties, said that they were of Christ. Therefore, they were severely rebuked by the Apostle Paul, who had led them to salvation and who had established them as the church. Paul called them to account, asking them whether Christ had been divided. Obviously Christ has not been and cannot be divided. However, those who had believed and had been baptized into Christ were divided one from another. This offended Christ, dividing His Body, separating the unique church, which He redeemed by shedding His blood, into many different sects.

Furthermore, the Apostle Paul asked the divided Corinthian believers, "Was Paul crucified for you? Or were you baptized into the name of Paul?" Of course not! Paul did not die to accomplish redemption for them; neither were they baptized into the name of Paul. It was Christ who died to accomplish redemption for them, and it was Christ into whom they had been baptized. Yet why did they say they were of Paul? This is just like some today who are redeemed by Christ and are baptized into Christ, who say that they are of Luther (the Lutheran sect), or of Wesley (the Wesleyan sect), or of the Baptist church (the Baptist sect), or of the Presbyterian church (the Presbyterian sect). Here Paul's rebuking and denouncing of the divisive Christians strongly condemn and deny all divisions, sects, and denominations in Christianity today.

II. THE BODY OF CHRIST BEING UNIQUE

1) "One Body and one Spirit...one Lord...one God" (Eph. 4:4-6).

Since Christ is not divided, neither should Christians who belong to Christ be divided into sects. Even the more, since the Body of Christ is unique, Christians who are members of this unique Body should not divide it into many different sects. We should only want the unique Body of Christ, not the many man-made sects. In this Body of Christ, there is only one Spirit; also, His Body has only one Lord, that is, one Head. Furthermore, all the members of His Body are regenerated by one God and Father, and they are indwelt by Him. The Triune God has been mingled with all the believers as one, and the essence of His divine oneness in the believers has further constituted them into an indivisible Body. The Spirit is the one life which they all possess. How can a body have two or more lives? The Lord is the one Head to whom they belong. How can a body have two or more heads? God is the one Father who begat them. How can the children of God have two or more Fathers? It is strange and unreasonable for a single body to have more than one life, or for a body to have more than one head, or for a family of children to have more than one father! Yet these unreasonable and strange things are actually being established, supported, respected, and promoted by a majority of Christians! None of the lovers of the Lord or those who know the Lord's heart and the truth of the Bible should do this. Rather, they should imitate the Apostle Paul to condemn and deny these things which offend Christ, sadden God, and grieve the Holy Spirit.

III. SECTS BEING OF THE FLESH

1) "And the works of the flesh are manifest, which are...faction, divisions, parties, envyings" (Gal. 5:19-21).

In Greek, the word for party or sect (*hairesis*) is the same as the word for heresy (*hairesis* anglicized), which means to label something new in order to be different, resulting in a distinctive party—a sect.

The verses here tell us clearly that sects come from men's flesh. They also show us that there are always factions and divisions before the formation of a sect, and envyings after its establishment. What a shame! Is this not the very condition among Christians today? Should we not refuse this work of the flesh by following the Holy Spirit in us who sanctifies us?

IV. REFUSING FACTIONS

1) "A factious man after a first and second admonition refuse" (Titus 3:10).

In confronting factions among the Christians, the Apostle Paul gave his younger co-worker a frank and bold charge, which is also a charge to us, to refuse a factious person after sufficient admonition in love. This is to reject factions without lenience or compromise according to God's heart's desire and the truth of the Bible that the Body of Christ may not suffer damage and that the truth of God may not be adulterated.

V. THE FACTORS CONSTITUTING SECTS

The following three key elements are the factors which

cause the Christians (not counting the nominal ones) to be divided, to be constituted as sects.

A. Special Creeds

The common faith of true Christians is unique. It includes the Triune God, the person and work of Christ, that is, the being of Christ and the doings of Christ, and the divine authority of the Bible. Besides these truths of our fundamental faith, to consider other matters to be the Christian faith (such as the method of baptism of the Baptist denomination, the system of church administration of the Presbyterian denomination, the tongue-speaking of the Pentecostal denomination, the head covering and foot washing of other groups, or general doctrines such as the time and number of raptures, the interpretation of prophecies, and the understanding of certain parts of the Scriptures) and to make them special creeds is to label something new in order to be different and will result in sects.

B. Special Fellowships

With the existence of special creeds, Christians will be divided into different groups, having special fellowships in their different circles outside of the believers' common fellowship. Such special fellowships cause those believers who practice them to be constituted as sects separate from the believers in general.

C. Special Names

Special creeds not only lead to special fellowships, but they also produce special names, such as the name of a certain denomination or a certain church. These special names, in a more tangible way, cause those who so label themselves to be constituted into named sects, resulting in denominations. A denomination is a named sect. Therefore, those who know the Body of Christ must never bear such special names. The believers should only possess the unique and honorable name of Jesus Christ, and not exalt any other name besides this preeminent name. It should not be a glorious thing for one to say that he is a believer of a certain denomination.

VI. ENDEAVORING TO KEEP THE ONENESS
OF THE BODY OF CHRIST

1) "I beseech you therefore, I, the prisoner in the Lord, to walk worthily of the calling with which you were called, with all lowliness and meekness, with longsuffering, bearing with one another in love, being diligent to keep the oneness of the Spirit [that is, the oneness of the Body of Christ] in the uniting bond of peace" (Eph. 4:1-3).

The Spirit, that is, the Holy Spirit who lives in us, causes us to be constituted into the Body of Christ with God's life. Since there is one Body, there is also one Holy Spirit who lives in the Body. This one Holy Spirit is the oneness in the one Body. If we believers would live in this Spirit and walk according to this Spirit, the oneness of the Body of Christ would be kept. Otherwise, that oneness would be broken. In the status of one imprisoned because of the church, the Apostle Paul beseeched us in Ephesians 4:2-3 to keep this oneness with such virtues as lowliness, meekness, longsuffering, bearing in love, and the uniting bond of peace, that our walk may be worthy of our calling. God's calling is that we would be members of the Body of Christ. If our walk damages and hurts the oneness of the Body of Christ, it is not worthy of God's calling. Therefore, we must endeavor to live in the Body of Christ to keep the oneness of the Body, not participating in any divisions, sects, or denominations.

THE CHURCH — THE LORD'S RECOVERY

Peculiar Meter. (*Hymns*, #1255)

1 We are for the Lord's re-cov-ery Of the lo-cal church; We are for the Lord's re-cov-ery Of the ci-ty and the earth. Stand-ing on the ground of one-ness, One-ness in the Lord, We are build-ing up the temple Of our glor-ious Lord. We are for the Lord's, We are for the Lord's, We are for the Lord's re-co-ve-ry! We are for the Lord's, We are for the Lord's, We are for the Lord's re-cov-ery!

2 We are for the Lord's recovery,
  To our hearts so dear;
When we exercise our spirit,
  Our vision is so clear.
Babylon the Great is fallen,
  Satan is cast down,
And the local church is builded
  On the local ground.

MEETINGS

(1)

Since the church is the assembly called out by God from the world, it should meet continually. Meetings enable God's called out congregation to be supplied, established, and perfected, that the goal of God's calling this assembly may be accomplished.

I. GOD'S ORDINATION FOR THE BELIEVERS

1) **"Not forsaking the assembling of ourselves together"** (Heb. 10:25).

Here the assembling of ourselves together refers to our Christian meetings. God has ordained the way in which every living thing in the universe should exist. God's ordination is the very law by which a particular species lives. If the living thing obeys that law, it will survive and be blessed. God is the same toward us who have believed in Christ. God's ordination for us, which becomes our law of existence and blessing, is the meetings. As water is to the fish, and air to the birds, so are the meetings to the Christians. As the fish must live in the water and the birds must exist in the air, so the Christians must maintain their spiritual existence and living by the meetings.

II. A REQUIREMENT OF THE SPIRITUAL LIFE

1) **"...sheep...be one flock"** (John 10:16).

Every kind of life has its own characteristic, and usually, many characteristics. The spiritual life we believers have received, being the life of God in us, also possesses many characteristics. For example, the hatred for sin and the separation from sin are characteristics of this life. The desire to draw near to God and the willingness to serve Him are also its characteristics. One of the many characteristics of our

spiritual life is to flock together, to meet together. John 10:3
and 16 show us that since we are saved, we are the Lord's
sheep. The characteristic of the sheep's life is to flock
together and to dislike isolation from the other sheep. Hence,
the Bible says that we are not only the Lord's sheep, but even
more, His flock (Acts 20:28; 1 Pet. 5:2). In order to be a sheep
which shares in the blessing of the flock, we must meet
together with the flock. The characteristic of the spiritual
"sheep life" within us requires this of us.

III. THE IMPORTANCE OF
THE BELIEVERS' MEETINGS

1) **"For where two or three are gathered together
into My name, there I am in their midst"** (Matt. 18:20).

Here the Lord especially promised that wherever two or
three of us who belong to Him are gathered together into
His name, that is, meet in His name, He is in our midst.
When we meet in His name, we enjoy His presence in a
special way. His very presence undoubtedly brings us
enlightenment, grace, supply, and all kinds of blessing.
How precious this is! What a blessing this is! We can only
enjoy such rich blessing by meeting together.

2) **"And rising up that very hour, they returned to
Jerusalem and found the eleven and those with them
assembled together...and as they were speaking
these things, He Himself [Jesus] stood in their midst
and said to them, Peace to you!"** (Luke 24:33-36).

This speaks of the two disciples who left Jerusalem to
go to Emmaus. On their way, when they discovered that it
was the Lord who had appeared to them, the Lord
disappeared from them. Immediately they returned to
Jerusalem, where they should have remained originally.
When they arrived, they found the apostles and those with
them assembled together, and the Lord appeared among
them. They and the apostles and the other disciples all
enjoyed the Lord's appearing and experienced the blessing
of the Lord's presence when He returned among the
disciples for the first time after His resurrection. This is
also an evidence of the importance of meetings.

3) "And when the day of Pentecost was being fulfilled, they were all together in the same place... and they were all filled with the Holy Spirit" (Acts 2:1-4).

After He ascended, the Lord Jesus sent the Holy Spirit. The Holy Spirit was poured upon the disciples when they were meeting together, and they were all filled with the Holy Spirit outwardly. The outpouring of the Holy Spirit at Pentecost was not upon the disciples who were by themselves. Rather it was upon those disciples who were meeting together. Anyone who did not participate in that meeting missed an unprecedented blessing outpoured from the heavens. Again, this shows us the importance of meetings.

4) "And let us consider one another for inciting to love and good works, not forsaking the assembling of ourselves together... but exhorting one another, and so much the more as you see the day [of the Lord's coming] drawing near" (Heb. 10:24-25).

What is mentioned here shows us that meetings can cause us to consider one another for inciting to love and to exhort one another for good works. This causes us to have spiritual fellowship with the saints to receive the life supply from them. Thus, we must not forsake the meetings, and so much the more as we know that the Lord will soon come back. Our Christian life is not like the life of a butterfly, which does well on its own; our life is like the sheep's life, requiring that we flock together and live a meeting life. Consequently, we need to meet, and the meetings are crucial to us.

MEETINGS — EXHIBITING CHRIST

8.8.8.6. with chorus. (*Hymns*, #864)

1 When-e'er we meet with Christ en-dued, The sur-plus of His plen - i - tude We

of - fer un - to God as food, And thus ex - hib - it Christ.

Let us ex - hib - it Christ, Let us ex - hib - it Christ; We'll

bring His sur - plus to the church And thus ex - hib - it Christ.

2 In Christ we live, by Christ we fight,
    On Christ we labor day and night,
  And with His surplus we unite
    To thus exhibit Christ.

3 Our life and all we are and do
    Is Christ Himself, the substance true,
  That every time we meet anew
    We may exhibit Christ.

4 In meetings Christ to God we bear
    And Christ with one another share,
  And Christ with God enjoying there,
    We thus exhibit Christ.

5 The risen Christ to God we bring,
    And Christ ascended offering,
  God's satisfaction answering,
    We thus exhibit Christ.

6 The center and reality,
    The atmosphere and ministry,
  Of all our meetings is that we
    May thus exhibit Christ.

7 The testimony and the prayer,
    And all the fellowship we share,
  The exercise of gifts, whate'er,
    Should just exhibit Christ.

8 The Father we would glorify,
    Exalting Christ the Son, thereby
  The meeting's purpose satisfy
    That we exhibit Christ.

LESSON FIFTEEN

MEETINGS

(2)

IV. THE DIFFERENT KINDS OF MEETINGS FOR BELIEVERS

A. Bread Breaking Meeting

1) "And on the first day of the week, when we gathered together to break bread" (Acts 20:7).

To break bread is to eat the Lord's supper, remembering the Lord who died for us (1 Cor. 11:20, 23-25). This should be the first kind of regular meeting for us who have been redeemed by the Lord's death. See the following two lessons for details.

B. Prayer Meeting

1) "If two of you agree on earth concerning anything, whatever they may ask, it shall come to them from My Father who is in the heavens. For where two or three are gathered together..." (Matt. 18:19-20).

Here the Lord is speaking concerning the prayer of a meeting. This kind of prayer is more powerful than the prayer of an individual, being able to bind on earth what has been bound in heaven, and to loose on earth what has been loosed in heaven (Matt. 18:18).

2) "These all were persevering with one accord in prayer, together with the women..." (Acts 1:14).

Here again, the prayer of a meeting is mentioned. It was this prayer that brought in the blessing of the outpouring of the Holy Spirit on the day of Pentecost.

3) "And when they heard this, they lifted up their voice with one accord to God and said... And as they

were beseeching, the place in which they were gathered was shaken, and they were all filled with the Holy Spirit, and spoke the word of God with boldness" (Acts 4:24-31).

It says here that in those days when the disciples were under persecution, they met together to pray with one accord. That kind of prayer caused them to be filled outwardly with the Holy Spirit and to speak the word of God with boldness.

4) "Prayer was being made fervently by the church to God concerning him" (Acts 12:5); "where [the house of Mary] a considerable number were assembled together praying" (12:12).

On the day when Peter was imprisoned, the church prayed fervently for him, and a considerable number were assembled together in a sister's house, praying for him specifically. That prayer caused God to perform a great miracle, delivering Peter out of prison.

C. Meeting for the Exercise of Spiritual Gifts and for Mutual Building Up

1) "Whenever you come together, each one has a psalm, has a teaching, has a revelation, has a tongue, has an interpretation. Let all things be done for building up" (1 Cor. 14:26).

The meeting mentioned here is for the exercise of spiritual gifts and for mutual building up. In this kind of meeting, there is not a special person doing a specific thing, but everyone is exercising the spiritual gifts; one has a psalm, one has a teaching, one has a revelation, one does this, and another does that. Each one may participate with the goal of building up and edifying others.

D. Meeting for Reading the Word

1) "And having gathered the multitude together, they handed them the letter [written by the apostles and the elders in Jerusalem]. And when they read it, they rejoiced at the consolation" (Acts 15:30-31).

Here it says that when Paul and his companions arrived in Antioch, they gathered the saints together to read to them the letter written by the apostles and the elders in Jerusalem under the leading of the Holy Spirit. Hence, we may also need to meet together occasionally to read the word of God in the Bible.

E. Meeting to Listen to Messages

1) **"When we gathered together ... Paul discoursed with them, about to go forth on the next day"** (Acts 20:7).

On that day, the believers in Troas met together to listen to Paul discoursing with them concerning the spiritual things of God, that they might be edified and established. Therefore, sometimes we should also meet to listen to spiritual messages spoken for God by the Lord's minister of the word that we may be edified and established.

V. HOW TO MEET

1) **"For where ... are gathered together into My name, there I am in their midst"** (Matt. 18:20).

The most crucial thing in the believers' meeting is to be gathered into the Lord's name. This means that we have to meet in the name of the Lord. Since we are the Lord's and were saved by His name, we should gather only into that name and meet in that name. We must not gather into and meet in any other name, whether it is the name of an individual, of a corporate body, of a mission, or of a denomination.

2) **"And [1] day by day, [2] continuing steadfastly [3] with one accord [4] in the temple and breaking bread [5] from house to house"** (Acts 2:46).

This verse reveals to us that we should, first, meet daily; second, meet steadfastly and continually; third, meet with one accord; fourth, meet in a large place (such as the temple); and fifth, meet from house to house, that is, meet in every home.

3) "The whole church comes together in one place" (1 Cor. 14:23).

On the one hand, the church should meet continually in the homes of the believers; on the other hand, sometimes it is also necessary for the whole church to come together in one place. Separate home meetings, which should be regular, and meetings in one place, which should be held according to need, both have their own benefits and flavor. Thus, the church should have regular separate home meetings and should gather together in one place as the need arises.

MEETINGS — CHRIST AS THE CENTER

10.10.10.10. (*Hymns*, #863)

1 In daily walk and in our meetings too, Christ is the
center, Christ is ev-'ry-thing; 'Tis not for form nor doc-trine good and
true, But 'tis for Christ a-lone we're gath-er-ing.

2 Christ is the way and Christ the light of life,
In Him we walk and by Him we are led;
Christ is the living water and the food;
Of Him we drink and we with Him are fed.

3 Christ is the truth, 'tis Him we testify,
Christ is the life, 'tis Him we minister;
Christ is the Lord, 'tis Him we magnify,
Christ is the Head, and we exalt Him here.

4 Christ is the All in all to God and man—
  With Him both we and God are satisfied;
  Christ, the reality within the Church—
  By Him are life and numbers multiplied.

5 By all the hymns and prayers we offer here,
  Christ the reality we would express;
  All the activities in fellowship—
  Christ thus in operation manifest.

6 'Tis in His Name we meet, in Spirit act,
  With nothing in our mind to formalize;
  'Tis by His pow'r we pray, in unction praise,
  And with Himself in spirit exercise.

7 All things forgetting, cleaving unto Christ,
  Applying Him until maturity;
  Let us count everything but loss for Him,
  For Him, our All in all, eternally.

THE BREAD BREAKING MEETING

(1)

1) "We gathered together to break bread..." (Acts 20:7).

2) "You come together...to eat the Lord's supper" (1 Cor. 11:20).

3) "You...partake of the table of the Lord..." (1 Cor. 10:21).

These three verses show us that the bread breaking meeting is a meeting in which the believers come together to eat the Lord's supper and attend the Lord's table. This meeting is divided into two parts, the first part for remembering the Lord and the latter part for worshipping the Father.

I. REMEMBERING THE LORD—WITH THE LORD AS THE CENTER

1) **"And having taken a loaf...He broke it, and gave it to them, saying, This is My body which is given for you; do this unto the remembrance of Me. And similarly the cup after they had dined"** (Luke 22:19-20).

The bread breaking meeting is not for anything other than remembering the Lord with the remembrance of the Lord as its center for the Lord's enjoyment. Everything in this meeting, whether hymn singing, prayer, Bible reading, or words of inspiration, should take the Lord as the center, speaking either concerning His person and work, His love and virtues, His living or suffering on the earth, or His honor or glory in heaven, that others may consider or realize these things in order to remember the Lord Himself. In such a meeting, we should think of the Lord in our

hearts and behold the Lord in our spirit that we would be
inspired concerning the Lord. Then we will express our
inspiration through songs, prayers, reading of the Bible, or
words, that the feeling of the entire meeting would be
directed to the Lord and that all would remember the Lord.

A. Eating the Lord's Supper

The three verses quoted in the beginning of this lesson
show us that the breaking of bread is to eat the Lord's supper
and to attend the Lord's table. Eating the Lord's supper is
for us to remember the Lord; attending the Lord's table
is for us to have fellowship together in the Lord's
accomplishments for us. In the aspect of eating the
Lord's supper, we should mainly do the following three things:

1. Remember the Lord

1) **"The Lord Jesus...took bread...broke it and
said, This is My body, which is for you; this do unto
the remembrance of Me"** (1 Cor. 11:23-24).

According to what the Lord has established, whenever
we break bread, there is not only a loaf of bread prepared
for us to break and eat, but next to the bread there is also a
cup prepared for us to receive and drink. By eating the
Lord's bread and drinking the Lord's cup, we eat the Lord's
supper in remembrance of the Lord. The bread and the cup
are both symbols. According to what the Lord said, the
bread signifies His body that He gave for us and the cup
signifies the blood that He shed for us. His body was given
for us on the cross and His blood was shed for us also on
the cross. He gave Himself for us in order to impart life
into us that we may partake of Him. He shed His blood for
us in order to redeem us that our sins may be forgiven.

When we see or receive the bread that we break, we should
consider how the Lord became flesh for us, how He died for us
in the flesh, and how His body was broken for us and given to
us that we may have His life. In the Bible, bread refers to life.
The Lord said that He is the bread of life which gives life to
the world (John 6:33-35). Whenever bread is mentioned, we
must think of life. The Lord's body being broken to be given

as bread to us means that He gave His body for us that we may have His life. We partake of His life when we receive His broken body. All of this is signified by our breaking of bread and by the bread which we break.

2) "Similarly also the cup after supper, saying, This cup is the new covenant in My blood; this do, as often as you drink it, unto the remembrance of Me" (1 Cor. 11:25).

In the bread breaking meeting, we should consider the Lord and what He did for us not only when we see or receive the bread which we break but also when we see or receive the cup which we drink. This cup signifies the new covenant, which the Lord enacted for us by shedding His blood. Whenever we see or receive this cup which we drink, we should consider how the Lord partook of flesh and blood for us (Heb. 2:14), how He not only gave His body for us that we may have His life, but how He also shed His blood for us that we may have the topmost blessing, that is, to be delivered from sin and obtain God and all that is of Him. By this symbol, we should consider how the Lord bore our sins, was made sin for us, and was judged and cursed for us, shedding His blood, which constitutes our cup of blessing, our eternal blessed portion. We should also consider how we are redeemed, forgiven, sanctified, justified, reconciled, and accepted by God through the Lord's blood; how it cleanses us from our sins and washes our conscience that we may come to God with boldness; how it speaks better things before God; and how it resists the attacks from the evil spirits for us that we may overcome the Devil who accuses us.

In the Bible, the bread denotes life and the cup signifies "portion," such as "Jehovah is the portion of...my cup" (Psa. 16:5). Originally we were sinful and evil, and the portion we deserved from God should have been the cup of God's wrath, that is, to go into the lake of fire to suffer the torment of eternal perdition (Rev. 14:10; 21:8). However, God made the Lord Jesus drink the cup of wrath for us on the cross (John 18:11). He received God's righteous judgment

for us and fully tasted the torment of perdition in the lake
of fire; He shed His blood to fully redeem us from our sins
and enacted the new covenant for us, giving us instead the
cup of salvation (Psa. 116:13) and becoming our cup (of
blessing) (Psa. 23:5). In this blessed cup of salvation, God
Himself and all that He has has become our portion, our
eternal blessed portion, and the portion of our cup.

2. Enjoy the Lord

1) "**Jesus took the bread...broke it and gave it to
the disciples, and said, Take, eat**" (Matt. 26:26); "**This
is My body which is given for you; do this unto the
remembrance of Me**" (Luke 22:19); "**And taking the
cup...He gave it to them, saying, Drink of it, all of
you; for this is My blood of the covenant**" (Matt. 26:27-
28); "**...which is being poured out for you**" (Luke
22:20); "**This do, as often as you drink it, unto the
remembrance of Me**" (1 Cor. 11:24-25).

Although the center of the breaking of bread is to
remember the Lord, such remembrance is not merely to
reflect on the Lord and all that He has done for us, but
even more to enjoy the Lord and all that He has
accomplished for us. The Lord said that our eating His
bread and drinking His cup is our remembrance of Him.
His bread and His cup signify His body and His blood.
Thus, to eat His bread and drink His cup are to eat His
body and drink His blood. The Lord's body and His blood
are He Himself given for us and the means by which He
accomplished all things for us. Furthermore, to eat and to
drink are not only to receive but also to enjoy. When we eat
the Lord's body and drink His blood, we not only receive
but also enjoy the Lord Himself and all that He has
accomplished for us by giving His body and shedding His
blood. To receive and enjoy the Lord in this way is to
remember Him. It is when we thus eat, drink, and enjoy
the Lord that we truly remember Him. This is the profound
meaning of eating the Lord's supper.

Our eating, drinking, and enjoying the Lord at His
supper are also our declaration and testimony. Our

declaration is that we are joined to the Lord and are mingled with Him, just as the bread becomes mingled with us after being received into our body. Our testimony is that we live by eating, drinking, and enjoying the Lord, taking Him as our life every day. When we break bread to eat and drink the Lord, we declare that the Lord, by giving His body and shedding His blood, has come into us to be joined to us. We also testify that, by receiving the body the Lord gave for us and the blood He shed for us, we have partaken of Him and all that He has accomplished for us, we have been joined to Him, and we live by Him as our life and our life supply. This is our declaration as well as our testimony when we break bread.

3. Display the Lord's Death

1) "For as often as you eat this bread and drink the cup, you declare the Lord's death until He comes" (1 Cor. 11:26).

The word "declare" in this verse has the meaning of showing and displaying. Whenever we eat the Lord's bread and drink His cup, we simultaneously remember the Lord and display His death. We remember the Lord, not His death. But while we are remembering the Lord, we display the Lord's death for ourselves, the angels, and all things to see. When we remember the Lord, the bread and the cup are displayed separately on the table. The bread refers to the Lord's body and the cup to His blood. Since the separation of the body and the blood signifies death, death is thus displayed. This is how we display the Lord's death when we break bread to remember Him.

The Scripture quoted here says that we should remember the Lord and display His death until He comes. This implies that when we break bread to remember the Lord and to display His death, at the same time we are waiting for His coming. This shows that we should display the Lord's death and thus remember Him in the spirit and atmosphere of waiting for His coming.

PRAISE OF THE LORD — REMEMBRANCE OF HIM

8.6.8.6. (*Hymns*, #220)

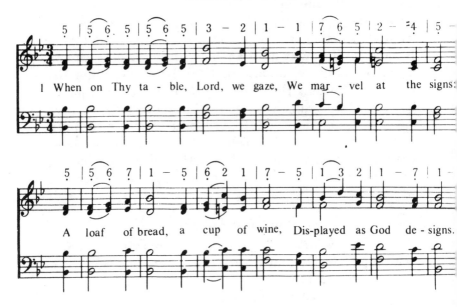

1 When on Thy ta - ble, Lord, we gaze, We mar - vel at the signs:
A loaf of bread, a cup of wine, Dis-played as God de - signs.

2 The loaf portrays the bread of life
As heav'nly food to us,
Imparted by Thy mystic death
That we may share Thee thus.

3 The portion is the cup divine,
Composed of Jesus' blood;
This cup of blessing we receive
And gain what is of God.

4 We eat of Thee, the Bread of life,
By sharing here this bread;
Thus we remember Thee in love
And with Thyself are fed.

5 We all enjoy the blessings gained
  By drinking of this cup;
Thus we remember Thee with joy,
  Till we are taken up.

6 By feasting on this bread and cup
  Thy death we now declare,
And testify Thou art our life
  And all we daily share.

7 We're waiting for that glorious hour,
  When in the fullest way
We'll feed on Thee and feast with Thee
  And worship Thee for aye.

THE BREAD BREAKING MEETING

(2)

B. Attending the Lord's Table

1) "The cup of blessing which we bless, is it not a fellowship of the blood of Christ? The bread which we break, is it not a fellowship of the body of Christ? Seeing that we who are many are one bread, one Body; for we all partake of the one bread" (1 Cor. 10:16-17).

First Corinthians 11:23-25 shows us that the emphasis in eating the Lord's supper is the remembrance of the Lord, whereas 1 Corinthians 10:16-17 and 21 tell us that the stress in attending the Lord's table is the fellowship with the saints.

In the bread breaking meeting, we are eating the one bread, which signifies the body of Christ, and drinking the one cup, which signifies the blood of Christ. Our eating and partaking of one bread and our drinking and sharing in one cup imply mutual fellowship. We have this fellowship because of the Lord's body and the Lord's blood. Hence, such fellowship becomes the fellowship of the blood of Christ and the fellowship of the body of Christ. In this way, when we eat and drink together, sharing in the Lord's bread and the Lord's cup, we "partake of the table of the Lord" (1 Cor. 10:21). At this table, we share in the Lord's body and the Lord's blood with all the saints and have fellowship one with another. The blood of Christ, which we enjoy together, removes all the barriers between the saints. The bread, which we share and which symbolizes the individual body of Christ, comes into us to make us one bread, signifying the one corporate Body of Christ. In the aspect of eating the Lord's supper, the bread refers to the Lord's individual body, which He gave for us on the cross, while in the aspect of attending the Lord's table, the bread points to the Lord's corporate Body, which He constituted with all the regenerated saints through His resurrection from the dead. The former is physical and was put to death and given for us; the latter is mystical and is constituted with all the saints in the Lord's resurrection. Therefore, each time that we break the bread, on the one hand we remember the Lord and enjoy Him by receiving the body which He gave for us on the cross; on the other hand, we enjoy the mystical Body which He produced through His resurrection from the dead, fellowshipping with all the saints in this mystical Body and testifying the oneness of this mystical Body. There is not only a relationship between us and the Lord, but a relationship between us and all the saints.

II. WORSHIPPING THE FATHER—
WITH THE FATHER AS THE CENTER

The meeting for the breaking of bread is a meeting for the believers' worship. According to the procedure in God's salvation, we first receive the Lord and then draw near to the Father. Thus, in this meeting for worship, we should first remember the Lord and then worship the Father. The center of the section of remembering the Lord is the remembrance of the Lord, and the center of the section of worshipping the Father is the worship of the Father, where all the prayers, hymns, and words should be directed toward the Father.

1) **"Jesus took the bread and blessed and broke it and gave it to the disciples, and said, Take, eat; this is My body. And taking the cup... He gave it to them, saying, Drink of it, all of you; for this is My blood of the covenant... and having sung a hymn, they went out to the Mount of Olives"** (Matt. 26:26-30).

On that day, after the Lord Jesus broke bread and sang a hymn with the disciples, He led them to the Mount of Olives to meet with the Father. A principle is implied and established here, that is, after we have broken the bread to remember the Lord, we ought to be led by Him to worship the Father together.

2) "I [the resurrected Christ] will declare Your [the Father's] name to My brothers; in the midst of the church [the meeting with the disciples after resurrection] I will sing hymns of praise unto You" (Heb. 2:12).

Here is mentioned what the Lord did when He appeared to and met with His disciples after His resurrection, that is, He considered them as brothers and declared to them the Father's name. He also considered them as the church and sang hymns of praise to the Father among them. Although the Lord is the only begotten Son of God, through death and resurrection, He regenerated us who believed in Him (1 Pet. 1:3) that we might become the many sons of God. He then became the firstborn Son of God (Rom. 8:29), leading us, who are the many sons, with Him to the Father. After He was resurrected, He came among the disciples (John 20:19-29) and declared the Father's name to His brothers. Then in the status of the firstborn Son of God, He led His many brothers, who are God's many sons, to sing praises to the Father together, that is, to worship the Father together. According to this fact, after we have broken the bread in remembrance of the Lord, we should be led by the Lord to worship the Father. In this section of the meeting, we take the Father as the center, and, as depicted in *Hymns*, #52, all our singing of praises to the Father is the Lord in us leading us to sing praises to the Father.

III. THE PERSONS WHO BREAK BREAD

1) "Jesus took the bread...and gave it to the disciples" (Matt. 26:26).

When the Lord established the breaking of bread, He gave the bread and the cup to His disciples, that is, to those who have believed into Him, have His life, and belong to Him. Of course, only those who have such a relationship with the Lord and who know the Lord as their personal Savior can remember the Lord by eating His bread and drinking His cup and can display the Lord's death by His bread and His cup.

2) "And all those who believed... breaking bread" (Acts 2:44-46).

Those who break bread must be "those who believed," that is, those who have believed and received the Lord's salvation, who have the Lord's life, and who belong to the Lord. Only such believing persons can and may break bread. Therefore, only those who are saved, who are joined unto the Lord, and who do not live in sin are qualified to eat the bread and drink the cup. No one else can have a share in the Lord's bread and the Lord's cup.

IV. THE TIME FOR THE BREAKING OF BREAD

1) "And they were continuing steadfastly... in the breaking of bread" (Acts 2:42).

Here it says that the early believers continued steadfastly in the breaking of bread; that is, they continued without ceasing to break bread all the time. We should follow such a pattern.

2) "And day by day... breaking bread" (Acts 2:46).

The early believers continued so steadfastly in the breaking of bread that they did it on a daily basis. At the time, because they were fervent toward the Lord and loved Him deeply, they spontaneously broke bread every day. This tells us that, if possible, the more often we break bread to remember the Lord the better.

3) "And on the first day of the week, when we gathered together to break bread" (Acts 20:7).

The early believers began by breaking bread daily. Later on, they gradually acquired the habit of doing it once a week on the first day. The first day of the week, which is the Lord's Day, is the day of the Lord's resurrection and the beginning of a new week, signifying that the old things are passed away and a new life has begun. Therefore, it is most appropriate to break bread to remember the Lord on this day. Furthermore, although we display the Lord's death when we break bread, we are actually remembering Him in resurrection.

4) "Eat the Lord's supper" (1 Cor. 11:20).

Since the breaking of bread is to eat the Lord's supper, it is best to conduct it in the evening. Furthermore, in the evening, having finished all our work and having discharged all our burdens, we are lightened in heart and refreshed in spirit. It is a proper time in which we can remember the Lord without anxiety, and it is easy to sense the Lord's presence then. This, however, is not a legal matter. If it is difficult or inconvenient to conduct it in the evening, we may evaluate the situation and change the time to the morning or the afternoon.

V. THE PLACE FOR THE BREAKING OF BREAD

1) "Breaking bread from house to house" (Acts 2:46).

The early believers broke bread from house to house in every home. It is clear that the place for the breaking of bread was their homes.

2) "When therefore you come together in the same place...to eat the Lord's supper" (1 Cor. 11:20).

According to this word, the early believers also came together in one place to eat the Lord's supper. This must have occurred in a larger place. There is the sweet and intimate flavor of a small meeting when we gather to break bread in the homes. There is also the rich and uplifted atmosphere of a large meeting when we gather together in one place. The believers may break bread in separate homes or in one place, and this should be decided on by the church according to the need and the situation.

VI. AFTER THE BREAKING OF BREAD

1) "For as often as you eat this bread and drink the cup, you declare the Lord's death until He comes" (1 Cor. 11:26).

Those who break bread to remember the Lord should be those who long for the Lord, wait for His coming, and love

His appearing (2 Tim. 4:8). Therefore, after we break bread, we ought to live a life of waiting for the Lord's coming.

2) "You cannot drink the cup of the Lord and the cup of demons; you cannot partake of the table of the Lord and of the table of demons" (1 Cor. 10:21).

Here it says that if we partake of the Lord's table, we cannot partake of the table of demons, and if we drink the Lord's cup, we cannot drink the cup of demons. According to the text preceding this verse, the table of demons and the cup of demons are the idol sacrifices. Thus, after we break bread, we cannot eat the idol sacrifices.

3) "Let us therefore keep the feast, not with old leaven, nor with leaven of malice and evil, but with unleavened bread of sincerity and truth" (1 Cor. 5:8).

Here, leaven refers to all evil and all that corrupts us. In the Old Testament, immediately after they kept the Passover, the Israelites observed the feast of unleavened bread, removing all leaven from their living (Deut. 16:1-4). The breaking of bread in the New Testament replaces the Passover in the Old Testament. Thus, after the breaking of bread, we should keep the feast of unleavened bread as the Israelites did, removing from our life all evil and all that corrupts us. We would only live a holy life free from sin by the Lord's holy and sinless life, which is the unleavened bread of sincerity and truth, to be those who truly keep the feast of unleavened bread.

PRAISE OF THE LORD — REMEMBRANCE OF HIM

8.7.8.7.D. with chorus. (*Hymns,* #221)

1 Lord, we thank Thee for the ta - ble, With the bread and with the wine.

At this ta - ble we en - joy Thee As the feast of love di - vine.

We par - take the bread, the em - blem Of Thy bod - y giv'n for us;

And we share the wine, the sym - bol Of Thy blood Thou shedd'st for us.

CHORUS

Lo, the ho - ly ta - ble! With the sa - cred sym - bols;

Its sig - nif - i - cance in fig - ure   Is un-search - a - ble!

2 By the death of Thy redemption,
   That Thy life Thou may impart,
E'en Thyself to us Thou gavest
   That we share in all Thou art.
By the bread and wine partaking,
   We Thy death display and prove;
Eating, drinking of Thyself, Lord,
   We remember Thee with love.

3 By this bread which signifieth
   Thy one body mystical,
We commune with all Thy members
   In one bond identical.
By this holy cup of blessing,
   Cup of wine which now we bless,
Of Thy blood we have communion
   With all those who faith possess.

4 Thou art our eternal portion,
   Here we take a sweet foretaste;
We are waiting for Thy kingdom,
   And Thy coming now we haste.
At Thy coming, in Thy kingdom,
   With all saints that overcome,
We anew will feast upon Thee
   And Thy loving Bride become.

CONSECRATING OURSELVES

For us, the saved persons, to consecrate ourselves is a positive reaction to the Lord's salvation. Since we have enjoyed the Lord's great and free salvation, we spontaneously desire to repay the Lord. When we consecrate ourselves to the Lord, we allow the Lord to gain us as our repayment to Him.

I. THE BASIS OF CONSECRATION

1) "You are not your own... For you were bought with a price; therefore glorify God in your body" (1 Cor. 6:19-20).

The basis of our consecration to the Lord is that, since He bought us with His blood as a price (Rev. 5:9), we have become His purchased slaves. We who believe in the Lord and who are redeemed and bought by the Lord are the purchased slaves of the Lord; we are not our own, but the Lord's. It is the Lord, not we, who has the right over us.

2) "For whether we live, we live to the Lord, or if we die, we die to the Lord. Therefore, whether we live or die, we are the Lord's" (Rom. 14:8).

Since we who are redeemed and bought by the Lord belong to Him, whether we live or die, we are the Lord's. This is the basis on which we consecrate ourselves to Him for His use.

II. THE MOTIVE OF CONSECRATION

1) "For the love of Christ constrains us, having judged this, that One died on behalf of all; therefore all died; and He died on behalf of all, that those who live may no longer live to themselves, but to Him who died for them and has been raised" (2 Cor. 5:14-15).

We consecrate ourselves to the Lord because His love confines and constrains us. His love compels us so that we cannot help but consecrate ourselves to Him. Since He died on our behalf, we all died; therefore, there is no need for us to die. Furthermore, He died that we may have His life to live to Him. Such love constrains us and compels us to love Him and consecrate ourselves to Him. This consecration is our gratitude for and repayment of His great love. His buying us with His precious blood to make us His purchased slaves is the basis on which we consecrate ourselves to Him. He died for us because of His love, and this love is the motive for us to consecrate ourselves to Him.

III. THE SIGNIFICANCE OF CONSECRATION

1) "I beg you therefore, brothers, through the compassions of God to present your bodies a living sacrifice...which is your most reasonable service" (Rom. 12:1).

When we consecrate ourselves to the Lord, we present ourselves to Him as a living sacrifice, unlike the people in the Old Testament who offered dead sacrifices to the Lord. As a living sacrifice that has been presented, we are holy, that is, we have separated ourselves unto the Lord for His use, and we are well-pleasing to God, satisfying His heart's desire.

2) "Command the children of Israel, and say unto them, My offering, and my bread for my sacrifices made by fire, for a sweet savor unto me...two lambs of the first year without spot day by day, for a continual burnt offering" (Num. 28:2-3).

In the Old Testament, God required that His people offer the burnt offering to Him daily for His food that He could be satisfied. This typifies that, in the New Testament, we who belong to God should offer ourselves as a burnt offering daily to God for His satisfaction. The difference is that the Old Testament people offered dead sacrifices, whereas we offer living sacrifices. Although the nature of the two are different, their significance is the same, that is, to be God's food for His satisfaction. To offer ourselves to the Lord is to be a sacrifice for His satisfaction. What matters is not what we do for the Lord, but that we satisfy Him. This is the real significance of our consecration to the Lord.

IV. THE PURPOSE OF CONSECRATION

1) "...no longer live to themselves, but to Him who died for them and has been raised" (2 Cor. 5:15).

The purpose of our consecration to the Lord is to live to Him. Living to Him is higher than living for Him. When we live for Him, we and He may still be two, but when we live to Him, we and He must become one. When we live to Him, we take Him not only as our life but also as our person. In all our living and actions, we should cooperate with Him and allow Him to live Himself through us.

2) "Present your bodies a living sacrifice" (Rom. 12:1).

When we consecrate ourselves to the Lord, as mentioned previously, we present ourselves to the Lord as a living sacrifice to satisfy His heart's desire. This is a significant purpose of our consecration to the Lord.

3) "Present your bodies...which is your most reasonable service" (Rom. 12:1).

To present ourselves as a living sacrifice to the Lord is a most reasonable service. Such service does not depend on our working for the Lord but on our satisfying God. This also should be a purpose of our consecration to the Lord.

4) "For we are His workmanship, created in Christ Jesus for good works, which God before prepared that we should walk in them" (Eph. 2:10).

We believers, who have been chosen and redeemed by God, are His workmanship, created in Christ Jesus for good works, which He has prepared for us to walk in. This requires our consent, which results in our offering ourselves to Him that He might work on us to complete His good works. This should be another purpose for which we consecrate ourselves to the Lord.

5) "For you were bought with a price; therefore glorify God in your body" (1 Cor. 6:20).

The consummate purpose of our consecration to the Lord is to glorify God, that is, to allow God to be lived out from us and expressed through us as a manifestation of His glory.

V. THE RESULT OF CONSECRATION

1) "Christ's slave...bought with a price" (1 Cor. 7:22-23).

The first result of our consecration to the Lord is that practically we become slaves bought by the Lord, submitting to His authority in all things.

2) "For we are His workmanship, created in Christ Jesus for good works" (Eph. 2:10).

We are God's workmanship under His molding, just as the clay vessel is molded in the hands of the potter (cf. Isa. 64:8). Another result of our consecration to the Lord is that the Lord has our consent to freely mold us.

3) "Present yourselves to God...and your members as weapons of righteousness to God. For sin shall not lord it over you" (Rom. 6:13-14); **"Present your members as slaves to righteousness unto sanctification"** (6:19).

When we present ourselves and our members to the Lord, there is still another result; that is, our members become weapons of and slaves to righteousness that we may be freed from sin, no longer being lorded over by sin, unto sanctification.

4) "The priest shall burn all on the altar, to be a burnt sacrifice, an offering made by fire, of a sweet savor unto Jehovah" (Lev. 1:9).

The result of offering a burnt sacrifice in the Old Testament was that the burnt offering became ashes before men and a sweet savor to God. If we present ourselves as a living burnt offering to the Lord, and if we are truly faithful to Him, we will be like ashes before men and a delightful savor to God.

CONSECRATION — CONSTRAINED BY THE LORD'S LOVE

6.6.6.6.8.6. (*Hymns*, #436)

1 Thy Life was giv'n for me, Thy blood, O Lord, was shed,

That I might ran-som'd be, And quick-en'd from the dead;

Thy Life was giv'n for me, for me; What have I giv'n for Thee?

2 Long years were spent for me
   In weariness and woe,
   That through eternity
   Thy glory I might know;
   Long years were spent for me,
      for me;
   Have I spent one for Thee?

3 Thy Father's home of light,
  Thy rainbow-circled throne,
  Were left for earthly night,
  For wanderings sad and lone;
  Yea, all was left for me, for me;
  Have I left aught for Thee?

4 Thou, Lord, hast borne for me
  More than my tongue can tell
  Of bitterest agony,
  To rescue me from hell;
  Thou suff'redst all for me, for me;
  What have I borne for Thee?

5 And Thou hast brought to me
  Down from Thy home above
  Salvation full and free,
  Thy pardon and Thy love;
  Great gifts, great gifts Thou
      broughtest me;
  What have I brought to Thee?

6 Oh, let my life be given,
  My years for Thee be spent;
  World-fetters all be riven,
  And joy with suff'ring blent;
  Thou gav'st Thyself for me, for me,
  I give myself to Thee.

CONSECRATION — POSSESSING ALL IN THE LORD

8.6.8.6.D. (*Hymns*, #473)

1 No mor - tal tongue can e'er de-scribe The free - dom of the
soul, When passed be - yond all earth - ly bribe To God's com - plete control. All things are his, yes, life, and death, Things pres-ent or to
come; In Christ he draws in peace each breath, In Christ he finds his home.

2 When such as we the King can choose,
  To share with Him His throne,
'Tis passing strange that we refuse
  To be our Lord's alone.
O never speak of sacrifice!
  A privilege untold
Is to be His at any price,
  In Calv'ry's hosts enrolled.

3 Arise! the holy bargain strike—
  The fragment for the whole—
All men and all events alike
  Must serve the ransomed soul.
All things are yours when you are His,
  And He and you are one;
A boundless life in Him there is,
  Whence doubt and fear are gone.

BEING FILLED INWARDLY AND OUTWARDLY WITH THE HOLY SPIRIT

(1)

We have already seen in lesson ten that the Holy Spirit is the ultimate expression of the Triune God and that He is the Triune God reaching and entering into the believers. Therefore, the Holy Spirit is for our experience of the Triune God. To experience the Triune God, we must have the practical experience of the Holy Spirit. A great part of our practical experience of the Holy Spirit is related to our being filled inwardly and outwardly with Him.

I. THE TWO ASPECTS OF THE HOLY SPIRIT

The Bible clearly shows us that the Holy Spirit is with us in two aspects.

A. The Significances of the Two Aspects

1. In

1) "The Spirit of reality...shall be in you" (John 14:17).

Here the Lord tells us clearly that the Holy Spirit will be in us.

2. Upon

1) "...the Holy Spirit has come upon you" (Acts 1:8).

On the one hand, the Lord spoke of the Holy Spirit being in us; on the other hand, He spoke of the Holy Spirit being upon us. To be upon us is outward and is absolutely different from being in us.

B. The Promises of the Two Aspects

1. The Lord Promising the "Comforter"—
Being Promised Before the Lord's Death

1) "And I will ask the Father, and He will give you another Comforter... even the Spirit of reality... shall be in you" (John 14:16-17); "If I go, I will send Him [the Comforter] to you" (John 16:7).

These are the words of the Lord before His, death, promising the disciples that He would go in order to send the Holy Spirit as the Comforter.

2. The Father Promising the "Power"—
Being Promised by the Father
in the Old Testament and Spoken of Again
by the Lord after His Resurrection

1) "I am sending forth the promise of My Father upon you... until you are clothed with power from on high" (Luke 24:49); "Wait for the promise of the Father... you shall receive power when the Holy Spirit has come upon you" (Acts 1:4-8).

The Lord spoke these words to the disciples after His resurrection and before His ascension, speaking again of God's promise in the Old Testament concerning the Holy Spirit. He promised that after He ascended to the heavens, He would send forth the Holy Spirit to be their power. The "power" is different from the "Comforter." The Comforter was the One who would enter into the disciples and be "in" them, while the power would come "upon" them. Thus, what the Lord said before His death and what He said after His resurrection are two different promises.

C. The Fulfillments of the Two Aspects

1. The Lord's Promise of the Comforter—
Being Fulfilled on the Evening
of the Day of Resurrection

1) "When therefore it was evening on that day, the first day of the week... Jesus came and stood in the midst... He breathed into them and said to them, Receive the Holy Spirit" (John 20:19-22).

This is the Lord, on the evening of the day of His resurrection, coming among the disciples and breathing into them for them to receive the Holy Spirit. This fulfills His promise made before His death concerning the Comforter.

2. The Father's Promise of Power— Being Fulfilled at Pentecost

1) "And when the day of Pentecost was being fulfilled, they were all together in the same place. And suddenly...out of heaven like a rushing violent wind, and it filled the whole house where they were sitting...and they were all filled with the Holy Spirit" (Acts 2:1-4).

This describes the coming of the Holy Spirit at Pentecost, fulfilling the promise of the Spirit of power, which was given by the Father and spoken of by the Lord to the disciples just before His ascension. Therefore, the Holy Spirit who descended was in the aspect of the power, not in the aspect of the Comforter, being different from what the Lord brought on the day of His resurrection. The Holy Spirit brought in on the day of resurrection is the "Comforter," and the Holy Spirit who descended at Pentecost is the "power."

D. The Functions of the Two Aspects

1. The Comforter Being for Life

1) "Comforter...may be with you...and shall be in you" (John 14:16-17).

It says here that the Holy Spirit as the Comforter is to be with us and in us. This speaks of the function of the Holy Spirit in the aspect of life. Therefore, the Comforter, that is, the Holy Spirit in the aspect of life, is for our inward life.

2. The Power Being for Work

1) "You shall receive power when the Holy Spirit has come upon you, and you shall be My witnesses..." (Acts 1:8).

It says here that the Holy Spirit's coming upon us is that we may have power to witness for the Lord. This shows us that the Holy Spirit's function as power is not for the life which we have inwardly from the Lord, but for the work which we do outwardly for the Lord. For our life within, God gives us the Holy Spirit as the Comforter, a Person to be our Lord within us, that inwardly He may be our life and the supplier and maintainer of our life. For our work without, God gives us the Holy Spirit as power that outwardly He may be for us to use as the power, authority, capability, and skill of our work.

E. The Symbols of the Two Aspects

1. Breath

1) "He breathed into them and said to them, Receive the Holy Spirit" (John 20:22).

This is the Lord's breathing of the Holy Spirit, who is the Comforter, as breath into the disciples on the evening of the day of resurrection. Breath is for life and signifies life. Thus, breath here is a symbol of the Holy Spirit as the inward Spirit of life.

2. Living Water

1) "Out of his innermost being shall flow rivers of living water. But this He said concerning the Spirit [the inward Holy Spirit of life], whom those who believed in Him were about to receive" (John 7:38-39).

The Lord's words here indicate to us that the Holy Spirit will flow out as the living water from within us. Surely this refers to the Holy Spirit as life within us, drunk by us as the living water to be our life supply. Therefore, the living water is also a symbol of the inward Spirit of life.

3. Wind

1) "A rushing violent wind...and they were all filled with the Holy Spirit" (Acts 2:2-4).

This is the disciples' receiving the Holy Spirit of power

upon them on the day of Pentecost in the upper room in Jerusalem. This is not like the breath breathed from within the Lord into them on the day of resurrection, but a rushing violent wind blowing upon them from without, signifying the Holy Spirit of power. Wind is naturally powerful and signifies power. Therefore, wind here is a sign of the Holy Spirit being the outward Spirit of power and is different from breath.

4. Mantle

1) "I am sending forth the promise [the outward Spirit of power] of My Father upon you...until you are clothed with power from on high" (Luke 24:49).

The Lord's word here also shows us that we are to be clothed outwardly with the Holy Spirit of power, promised by the Father, as a mantle worn by us to be our power. This is typified by the mantle Elisha received from Elijah (2 Kings 2:13-14). Therefore, this mantle is also a sign of the outward Holy Spirit of power and is different from the living water. This mantle Spirit, like the uniform of a public servant, brings authority and is useful for us to execute God's commission. The inward Spirit of life is the living water, which we can drink for our inward supply; the outward Holy Spirit of power is the mantle, which we can wear for our outward authority.

F. The Experiences of the Two Aspects

1. That of the Lord Jesus

1) "That which is begotten in her [Jesus] is of the Holy Spirit" (Matt. 1:20).

The Lord Jesus was conceived and born of the Holy Spirit. The life within Him is altogether the element of the Holy Spirit.

2) "And having been baptized...the Spirit of God descending as a dove and coming upon Him" (Matt. 3:16).

Although the Lord Jesus was conceived and born of the Holy Spirit, and the life within Him was totally the element of the Holy Spirit, He experienced the Holy Spirit coming upon Him to be His power to work for God only after He was baptized.

2. That of the Disciples

1) "It was evening on that day, the first day of the week...Jesus came and stood in the midst...He breathed into them and said to them, Receive the Holy Spirit" (John 20:19-22).

By the breath the Lord breathed into the disciples on the evening of the day of resurrection, the disciples received the Holy Spirit into them.

2) "And when the day of Pentecost was being fulfilled, they were all together in the same place... out of heaven like a rushing violent wind"; "...the Holy Spirit has come upon you" (Acts 2:1-4; 1:8).

Although the disciples had received the Holy Spirit into them on the evening of the day of resurrection, the Holy Spirit still came upon them on the day of Pentecost

FULLNESS OF THE SPIRIT — THE TWO ASPECTS

11.11.11.11. (*Hymns*, #278)

2 The Spirit of pow'r comes upon us today,
Who's likened to clothing ourselves to array;
In Him we are baptized, with Him we are dressed,
For service equipping with power possessed.

3 The Spirit of life is as breath glorious,
As spirit of life it is breathed into us;
The Spirit of pow'r doth the wind typify,
Which bloweth upon us with pow'r from on high.

4 Into His disciples the risen Lord breathed,
The Spirit of life thus to them He bequeathed;
Th' ascended Lord poured at the Pentecost hour
Upon His disciples the Spirit of pow'r.

5 The Spirit of life is within as the life,
The Spirit of power is giv'n for this life;
As blowing of wind brings the fresh air to breathe,
The Spirit of power to life doth bequeath.

6 These are not two spirits apart and afar,
But of the one Spirit the two functions are,
To clothe us with God and to fill us within,
That we may be thoroughly mingled with Him.

7 Lord, fill with Thy Spirit of life every part,
That we may grow up in Thy life as Thou art;
And clothe us without with Thy Spirit of pow'r
Thy will to fulfill in Thy service each hour.

BEING FILLED INWARDLY AND OUTWARDLY WITH THE HOLY SPIRIT

(2)

II. THE INWARD FILLING OF THE HOLY SPIRIT

To us the Holy Spirit is of two aspects—the inward aspect and the outward; therefore, to us there is also the inward filling and outward filling of the Holy Spirit. The New Testament uses two different words in its original language to describe the inward filling and the outward filling of the Holy Spirit. Speaking of the inward filling of the Holy Spirit, it uses the word *pleroo*, and speaking of the outward filling of the Holy Spirit, it uses the word *pletho*. First, we will look at the inward filling of the Holy Spirit.

A. The Fact of the Inward Filling of the Holy Spirit

1) "And the disciples were made full of joy and of the Holy Spirit" (Acts 13:52).

This verse speaks of the disciples being filled with the Holy Spirit inwardly. This Spirit who fills us is for life and living, since He is mentioned together with joy in the daily life.

B. The Function of the Inward Filling of the Holy Spirit

1) Being for the spiritual living that the spiritual life may mature—The inward filling of the Spirit is for our spiritual living that our spiritual life may mature. We may prove this with Acts 13:52, quoted previously, where joy and the Holy Spirit are mentioned together.

C. The Condition of the Believers After Being Filled Inwardly with the Holy Spirit— "Full of" the Holy Spirit

After we have been filled inwardly with the Holy Spirit, we are full of the Holy Spirit within. In the original language, "full of" is *pleres*, an adjective. To be filled with the Spirit is a procedure and should take place time after time, whereas to be full of the Spirit is a condition which results from such a procedure and should be constant.

1) "Select seven well-attested men from among you, full of the Spirit and of wisdom" (Acts 6:3).

At Pentecost the communal living of the church made it necessary for some to serve tables, and thus seven men full of the Spirit and of wisdom were chosen. The Holy Spirit and wisdom being mentioned here together proves that the Holy Spirit is for life and living. The service of the tables was cumbersome, which required men with a proper life and a spiritual living. They had to be persons full of the Holy Spirit.

2) "Stephen, a man full of faith and of the Holy Spirit" (Acts 6:5).

It tells us here that Stephen was a man full of faith and of the Holy Spirit. He was not only occasionally filled with the Holy Spirit, but a man always full of the Holy Spirit. Therefore, he had not only an abundant life and wisdom to serve many tables, but also an overcoming life and faith to stand for the Lord unto death (Acts 7:59-60).

3) "But [Stephen] being full of the Holy Spirit" (Acts 7:55).

Stephen maintained his condition of being full of the Holy Spirit. Although his persecutors hated him and gnashed their teeth at him, he was still full of the Holy Spirit. Hence, he was able to be faithful unto death, suffering martyrdom for the Lord's sake.

4) "For he [Barnabas] was a good man and full of the Holy Spirit and of faith" (Acts 11:24).

Barnabas was also full of the Holy Spirit, and that was why he could be a good man, full of faith.

D. The Manifestation of the Believers Being Filled Inwardly with the Holy Spirit

1. The Expression of Life

1) "Out of his innermost being shall flow rivers of living water. But this He said concerning the Spirit, whom those who believed in Him were about to receive" (John 7:38-39).

Since the Holy Spirit in us is the Spirit of life, and since our being filled inwardly with the Holy Spirit is for the maturity in life, the manifestation of being filled inwardly with the Holy Spirit must be an abundant, overflowing expression of life, flowing as rivers of living water out of our innermost being.

2. The Fruit of the Spirit

1) "But the fruit of the Spirit is love, joy, peace, longsuffering, kindness, goodness, faithfulness, meekness, self-control" (Gal. 5:22-23).

The fruit of life borne by the Holy Spirit from within us, such as the different virtues listed in these verses, is also a manifestation of our being filled with the Holy Spirit.

E. The Way to Be Filled Inwardly with the Holy Spirit

1. Receiving the Co-death with Christ on the Cross

1) "The flesh lusts against the Spirit...crucified the flesh" (Gal. 5:17-24).

Our flesh lusts against the Spirit. Therefore, in order to be filled with the Holy Spirit, we must first receive the dealing with our flesh through our co-death with Christ on the cross. It is only when we put the flesh and all that is of the flesh to death in Christ's death on the cross, not allowing the flesh and all that is of the flesh to have any place in us, that the Holy Spirit can gain ground in us, fully possessing us and filling us.

2. Offering Ourselves Fully to the Lord

After we have received the cross's dealing with the flesh, we still need to consecrate ourselves fully to the Lord for His use, at which time the Spirit of the Lord will possess us and fill us.

3. Believing the Filling of the Holy Spirit in Us

After we have dealt with the flesh and consecrated ourselves, we must then believe that:

1) **The Holy Spirit will fill us**—the Holy Spirit already lives in us, longs to fill us, and is waiting for us to give Him the ground. Now that we have thoroughly dealt with ourselves, giving all the ground to Him, He will surely come and fill us.

2) **The Holy Spirit has filled us**—since the Holy Spirit lives in us and longs and waits to fill us, once we empty ourselves and offer ourselves to Him, not only will He fill us, but He has already filled us. This is because once we are emptied and consecrated, He immediately fills us. This is not based upon feeling but based upon faith. Even if there is feeling, faith is still first, followed by the feeling.

4. Walking according to Spirit

1) **"Do not walk according to flesh, but according to spirit... mind... the things of the Spirit"** (Rom. 8:4-5).

After we have received the dealing of the cross, consecrated ourselves, and believed, we still must walk according to spirit and not according to flesh, and we must mind the things of the Spirit. Thus, the Holy Spirit will possess and fill us within.

2) **"Walk by the Spirit"** (Gal. 5:16, 25).

If we truly walk according to spirit, we will surely walk by the Spirit, not doing anything by the flesh or by depending on the strength of the flesh. In this way, we not only can be filled with the Holy Spirit instantly, but we also can be full of the Holy Spirit constantly.

FULLNESS OF THE SPIRIT — THE FILLING

8.7.8.7. with chorus. (*Hymns*, #1360)

1 O how glorious! O how precious! Now the Spirit dwells in me

Light im-part-ing, truth re-veal-ing, Shin-ing, lead-ing con-stant-ly.

CHORUS

Fill me now! Fill me now! Fill me with Thy Spir-it now

Strip me whol-ly, emp-ty thorough-ly, Fill me with Thy Spir-it now

2 Word of promise, real within me,
   Life divine now freeing me—
 From sin's cruel control releasing,
   From death's power setting free.

3 Deepest springs of life dispensing,
   Like the hart I thirst for Thee;
 Desp'rate, may I drink Thy fullness
   Till Thy river flows through me.

4 May my self be put to death, Lord,
   Under Thy control I'd be,
 Transformed to Thy living image,
   I'd forever flow out Thee.

FULLNESS OF THE SPIRIT — THE FILLING

8.7.8.7.D. (*Hymns*, #268)

1 How I praise Thee, precious Savior, That Thy love laid hold of me;

Thou hast saved and cleansed and filled me, That I might Thy chan-nel be.

CHORUS

Chan - nels on - ly, bless - ed Mas - ter, But with all Thy won-drous grace

Flow - ing through us, Thou canst use us Ev - 'ry hour in ev - 'ry place.

2 Just a channel, full of blessing,
   To the thirsty hearts around;
   To tell out Thy full salvation,
   All Thy loving message sound.

3 Emptied that Thou shouldest fill me,
   A clean vessel in Thine hand;
   With no strength but as Thou givest
   Graciously with each command.

4 Witnessing Thy grace to save me,
   Setting free from self and sin;
   Thou hast bought me to possess me,
   In Thy fulness, Lord, come in.

5 O Lord, fill now with Thy Spirit
   Hearts that full surrender know;
   That the streams of living water
   From our inner man may flow.

BEING FILLED INWARDLY AND OUTWARDLY WITH THE HOLY SPIRIT

(3)

III. THE OUTWARD FILLING OF THE HOLY SPIRIT

The believers have the need of both the inward life and the outward power. The Holy Spirit of God in His two aspects meets this twofold need of the believers. The consummate work of the inward Holy Spirit of life in the believers is to fill the believers inwardly in the aspect of life that they may live a spiritual and overcoming life. The primary work of the outward Holy Spirit of power on the believers is to fill the believers outwardly in the aspect of work that they may carry out a work of authority for the Lord. Therefore, we need to be filled with the Holy Spirit inwardly and outwardly.

A. The Baptism in the Holy Spirit

The Bible clearly shows us that the outward filling of the Holy Spirit is the baptism in the Holy Spirit.

1. The Prophecy

1) That of John the Baptist—"He [Christ] shall baptize you in the Holy Spirit" (Matt. 3:11). The first person to mention the baptism in the Holy Spirit was John the Baptist. When he came out to baptize people into water, he prophesied to them that the Lord Jesus would baptize people in the Holy Spirit that they might receive the Spirit baptism.

2) That of the Lord Jesus—"But you shall be baptized in the Holy Spirit not many days from

now" (Acts 1:5). This is the Lord's prophecy to the disciples after His resurrection and before His ascension based on the prophecy of John the Baptist.

2. The Fulfillment

1) For the Jewish believers on the day of Pentecost, on the one hand—"But you [the first group of Jewish believers] shall be baptized in the Holy Spirit not many days from now" (Acts 1:5); "And when the day of Pentecost was being fulfilled, they were all together in the same place...a rushing violent wind, and it filled the whole house where they were sitting...and they were all filled with the Holy Spirit" (Acts 2:1-4). The prophecies of John the Baptist and of the Lord Jesus concerning the baptism in the Holy Spirit began to be fulfilled on the day of Pentecost. According to the Bible, this fulfillment was divided into two parts. The first part was fulfilled in one place, while the second part was fulfilled in another place. Although it was divided into two parts and was fulfilled in two places, it was one complete fulfillment. It was separately fulfilled in two parts because the church is composed of two peoples, the Jews and the Gentiles. As depicted in these verses, the first part was fulfilled among the first group of representative Jewish believers in the upper room in Jerusalem on the day of Pentecost.

2) For the Gentile believers in the house of Cornelius, on the other hand—"Now as I [Peter] began to speak, the Holy Spirit fell on them [the Gentile believers] just as also on us [the first group of Jewish believers] at the beginning. And I remembered the word of the Lord, how He said...you shall be baptized in the Holy Spirit" (Acts 11:15-16). The second part of the baptism in the Holy Spirit was fulfilled in the house of Cornelius, being accomplished upon the representative Gentile believers, as described in these verses. According to the principle of representation, just as the Lord baptized all the Jewish believers throughout the

ages in the Holy Spirit once and for all on the day of Pentecost, likewise, He baptized all the Gentile believers throughout the ages in the Holy Spirit once and for all in the house of Cornelius. From God's view, as all the Jewish believers throughout the ages received the baptism in the Spirit on the day of Pentecost, in the same manner, all the Gentile believers throughout the ages received the baptism in the Spirit in Cornelius' house. These two parts of the baptism in the Spirit combine to form one complete baptism in the Spirit. It is in such a complete baptism in the Spirit that Christ the Head baptized all of us who believed into Him, whether Jews or Gentiles (represented by the Greeks), in one Holy Spirit into one Body (1 Cor. 12:13).

3. The Fact

1) **Being baptized in the Holy Spirit upon believing—"For also in one Spirit we were all baptized into one body, whether Jews or Greeks"** (1 Cor. 12:13). Since Christ baptized all the believers throughout the ages in the Holy Spirit on the day of Pentecost and in the house of Cornelius, He has already accomplished the baptism of the church in the Spirit through these two instances. The baptism in the Holy Spirit is a fact already accomplished upon the church. Today, when a Jew or a Gentile believes in the Lord, he participates in the church and hence participates in this accomplished fact upon the church. We who have believed into the Lord and belong to the church are not baptized one by one and time after time in the Holy Spirit; rather, we have received the entire baptism in the Spirit, which includes all the believers and is once for all.

4. The Experience

1) **To be filled outwardly with the Holy Spirit is to experience the baptism in the Holy Spirit—"But you shall be baptized in the Holy Spirit not many days from now"** (Acts 1:5); **"And when the day of Pentecost was being fulfilled...they were all filled**

with the Holy Spirit" (Acts 2:1-4); "The Holy Spirit
fell on them... And I remembered the word of the
Lord, how He said... you shall be baptized in the
Holy Spirit" (Acts 11:15-16). These verses show us that
both on the day of Pentecost and in the house of Cornelius,
to be baptized in the Spirit was to experience the outward
filling of the Holy Spirit. Thus, when we are filled
outwardly with the Holy Spirit, with the Holy Spirit of
power coming upon us, we experience the baptism in the
Spirit.

2) The fact of the baptism in the Holy Spirit was
accomplished once and for all upon the church
on the day of Pentecost and in the house of Cornelius;
however, the experience of the baptism in the Holy
Spirit is instant and numerous upon the believers—
The fact of the baptism in the Spirit has been accomplished
once for all upon the church. The experience of the baptism
in the Spirit takes place on the individual believers and is
instant and numerous. A believer can receive the fact of
the baptism in the Spirit only once, but he may experience
the baptism in the Spirit many times.

B. The Function of the Outward Filling of the Holy Spirit

1. For Spiritual Work That It May Be Powerful

1) "But you shall receive power when the Holy
Spirit has come upon you, and you shall be My
witnesses... unto the remotest part of the earth"
(Acts 1:8); "And when the day of Pentecost was being
fulfilled... they were all filled with the Holy Spirit"
(Acts 2:1-4).

The inward filling of the Holy Spirit is for spiritual
living that the spiritual life may mature, whereas the
outward filling with the Holy Spirit is for spiritual work
that the spiritual work may be powerful. To be merely
filled inwardly with the Holy Spirit is adequate for life, but
not for work. Before Pentecost, although Peter and the

early apostles were filled with the Holy Spirit inwardly, they were not able to work for the Lord because they had not yet been filled with the Holy Spirit outwardly in order to receive power to work for the Lord. It was when they were filled with the Holy Spirit outwardly at Pentecost and received the Holy Spirit coming upon them as the Spirit of power that they were empowered to do an exceedingly effective work for the Lord.

2. For Confirming That the Lord Jesus Has Ascended and Has Been Appointed both Lord and Christ

1) "Therefore having been exalted to the right hand of God, and having received...the Holy Spirit from the Father, He poured out this which you both see and hear...Therefore...know assuredly that God has made Him both Lord and Christ—this Jesus whom you crucified" (Acts 2:33-36).

The outward filling of the Holy Spirit also confirms to us the Lord's ascension and exaltation and His being appointed both Lord and Christ. The outward filling of the Holy Spirit is able to empower us because it brings the heavenly scene to us. The Holy Spirit, who fills us outwardly, is poured down by the ascended Lord and therefore brings us the heavens and the scene of the Lord in the heavens, giving us the sense that the heavens are very near and that the heavenly scene has fallen right before us. Since the scene of the Lord Jesus' being exalted and glorified on the heavenly throne seems to appear before us, we are able to witness for the Lord in the heavens by the heavenly power, not caring for the earthly situation and difficulties.

C. The Manifestation of the Outward Filling of the Holy Spirit

1) Speaking in tongues (Acts 2:4; 10:44-46; 19:6). Three groups of people—the disciples at Pentecost, the people in the house of Cornelius, and the disciples in Ephesus—spoke in tongues when they were filled

with the Holy Spirit outwardly. Thus, tongue-speaking is a manifestation of the outward filling with the Holy Spirit.

2) **Prophesying** (Acts 19:6). While being filled with the Holy Spirit outwardly, the believers in Ephesus not only spoke in tongues, but they also prophesied. Therefore, prophesying is also a manifestation of being filled with the Holy Spirit outwardly.

Of the many cases of the outward filling with the Holy Spirit recorded in the Acts of the Apostles, only three cases involving the three groups of people mentioned above had the speaking in tongues. In the other cases, the Bible does not mention tongue-speaking at all. This proves that speaking in tongues is not a necessary manifestation of the outward filling with the Holy Spirit.

3) **Having boldness and power—"And they were all filled with the Holy Spirit, and spoke the word of God with boldness"** (Acts 4:31); **"Then Peter, filled with the Holy Spirit, said to them..."** (Acts 4:8). To speak for God with boldness and power is also a strong manifestation of the outward filling with the Holy Spirit. The outward filling with the Holy Spirit is mainly for men to speak for God with boldness and power.

4) **Having authority—"Paul, filled with the Holy Spirit, looked intently at him and said, O son of the Devil, full of all deceit and all villainy, enemy of all righteousness...perverting the straight ways of the Lord...And now, behold, the hand of the Lord is upon you, and you will be blind, not seeing the sun for a time. And instantly a mist and a darkness fell upon him"** (Acts 13:9-11). This word shows us that when the Apostle Paul was outwardly filled with the Holy Spirit, he had the authority to deal with the evil person utilized by the Devil. This kind of authority is also a manifestation of the outward filling of the Holy Spirit.

D. The Way to be Filled
with the Holy Spirit Outwardly

**1) Repenting and dealing with sins—"Repent...
for the forgiveness of your sins, and you shall
receive the gift of the Holy Spirit"** (Acts 2:38).
Repentance for the forgiveness of sins will cause us to
receive the Holy Spirit. Hence, to be filled with the Holy
Spirit outwardly, there is the need for thorough repentance
and dealing with all sins.

**2) Believing—Believing that at the moment a
person believes into the Lord, he is baptized in the
Holy Spirit.** After we have fully dealt with our sins, we
have to believe that since the baptism in the Spirit is a fact
accomplished by the Lord on the church and that since we
are a part of the church, the outward filling with the Holy
Spirit from the baptism in the Spirit is now our portion.

**3) Obeying—"The Holy Spirit also, whom God
has given to those who obey Him"** (Acts 5:32). The
Holy Spirit is given by God to those who are obedient.
Therefore, to receive the outward filling of the Holy Spirit,
we must obey God.

**4) Praying with one accord—"These [who were to
be filled outwardly with the Holy Spirit at Pen-
tecost]† all were persevering with one accord in
prayer"** (Acts 1:14). In order to receive the outward filling
of the Holy Spirit, there is the need for much individual
prayer as well as prayer in one accord with those who
pursue the Lord together. This is what the first group of
people who received the outward filling with the Holy
Spirit did at Pentecost.

THE FULLNESS OF THE SPIRIT —
THE BAPTISM OF THE SPIRIT

Peculiar Meter. (*Hymns*, #273)

I Lord, we come to Thee, and with lib - er - ty Claim we now from Thee pow'r of might; For Thy king-dom's sake, may we pow'r par-take, Sit-ting in the heav - en - lies to fight. Pow - er! pow - er! clothe us with Thy pow-er! With Thy might-y pow-er from on high! Pow -er!

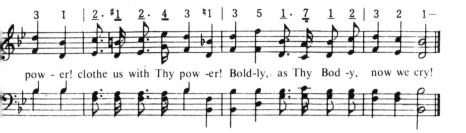

pow - er! clothe us with Thy pow -er! Bold-ly,. as Thy Bod -y, now we cry!

2 Lord, we look to Thee and with certainty
  Claim we now from Thee show'r divine.
For Thy Body's sake, may we show'r partake,
  Thus be fitted for the work of Thine.

  Shower! shower! pour on us Thy shower!
  Pour Thy heav'nly shower from on high!
  Shower! shower! pour on us Thy shower!
  Boldly, as Thy Body, now we cry!

3 Lord, we wait on Thee, and with surety
  Claim we now from Thee fire divine.
For Thy gospel's sake, may we fire partake,
  That the people's heart Thou may refine.

  Fire! fire! give us tongues of fire!
  To proclaim Thy message from on high!
  Fire! fire! give us tongues of fire!
  Boldly, as Thy Body, now we cry!

PREACHING THE GOSPEL

Every saved person, having believed into the Lord, must preach the gospel and delights to preach the gospel. The life of God in us, which we have received, is such a life. The more we preach the gospel, the more this life is released, and we will grow accordingly.

I. WHAT THE GOSPEL IS

1) **Being the glad tidings, the good news—"Him that bringeth good tidings... that publisheth salvation"** (Isa. 52:7); **"Those who announce glad tidings of good things!"** (Rom. 10:15). The gospel is the glad tidings and the good news of great joy, which God asked His servants to announce to men.

II. THE CONTENT OF THE GOSPEL

1) **Jesus Christ—"Bringing the good news of Jesus as the Christ"** (Acts 5:42). The chief content of the gospel is Jesus Christ, the Son of God (John 20:31). He is the One who is both God and man (Rom. 1:1-4), who has become the sinners' Savior (Matt. 1:21).

2) **"The gospel which I preached to you... that Christ died for our sins according to the Scriptures; and that He was buried, and that He has been raised on the third day according to the Scriptures"** (1 Cor. 15:1-4). Christ's death, by which He bore our sins, His burial, and His resurrection are also the main contents of the gospel. What Christ is, His person as the God-man, and what Christ has done, His work of redemption, constitute the contents of the gospel.

III. OTHER DESIGNATIONS OF GOSPEL PREACHING

1) **Witnessing—"Be My witnesses... unto the remotest part of the earth"** (Acts 1:8).

2) **Leading people to the Lord—"Andrew ... found first his own brother Simon ... He led him to Jesus"** (John 1:40-42).

3) **Sowing—"Gathers fruit unto eternal life, that he who sows and he who reaps may rejoice together"** (John 4:36).

4) **Reaping the harvest—"Beseech the Lord of the harvest that He may thrust out workers into His harvest"** (Matt. 9:38).

5) **Paying a debt—"I am debtor ... to [men] ... I am ready to preach the gospel to you"** (Rom. 1:14-15).

6) **Fruit-bearing—"I [the Lord] chose you, and I appointed you that you should go forth and bear fruit"** (John 15:16).

In the foregoing six portions of the Scripture, witnessing for the Lord, leading people to the Lord, sowing, reaping the harvest, paying a debt, and fruit-bearing are the other designations of gospel preaching.

IV. THE LORD'S CHARGE

1) **"Go therefore and disciple all the nations, baptizing them into the name of the Father and of the Son and of the Holy Spirit"** (Matt. 28:19).

2) **"Go into all the world and preach the gospel to all the creation"** (Mark 16:15).

After the Lord Jesus accomplished the redemption God had planned for His chosen people through His death and resurrection, and when He was about to leave the earth and ascend into heaven, He charged His disciples to go into all the world and preach the gospel to all the creation, discipling all the nations and baptizing them into the Triune God. This is a solemn charge. It was given not only to the disciples who were with the Lord but also to all those who have believed into Him and have been saved throughout the generations. We must, therefore, receive seriously this charge to go and spread the Lord's gospel.

V. THE SPIRIT OF GOSPEL PREACHING— REVEALING THE ATTITUDE IN PREACHING THE GOSPEL

1) **Burning in spirit**—"Being fervent in spirit, he was speaking and teaching accurately the things concerning Jesus" (Acts 18:25).

2) **Being provoked in spirit**—"His spirit was provoked in him as he beheld that the city was full of idols" (Acts 17:16).

3) **Not being ashamed**—"For I am not ashamed of the gospel; for it is the power of God unto salvation to every one..." (Rom. 1:16).

4) **Willing to sacrifice our status**—"For though I am free from all, I have enslaved myself to all, that I might gain the more...To the weak I became weak, that I might gain the weak. To all men I have become all things, that I might by all means save some. And I do all things for the sake of the gospel, that I may become a fellow partaker of it" (1 Cor. 9:19-23).

5) **Gladly spending and being spent**—"But I will most gladly spend and be utterly spent on behalf of your souls" (2 Cor. 12:15).

6) **Not being afraid of suffering evil**—"Suffer evil with the gospel according to the power of God" (2 Tim. 1:8).

7) **Leaving all**—"One who has left house or brothers or sisters or mother or father or children or fields for My [the Lord's] sake and for the gospel's sake" (Mark 10:29).

Burning in spirit, being provoked in spirit, not being ashamed of the gospel, willing to sacrifice one's status, gladly spending and being spent, not being afraid of suffering evil, and leaving all, as mentioned above, are the attitudes we should have in preaching the gospel. May the Lord give us grace that we may imitate the beautiful and excellent patterns of the early saints.

VI. THE PERSONS WHO PREACH
THE GOSPEL

1) Being worthy of the Lord's gospel—"Conduct yourselves worthily of the gospel of Christ" (Phil. 1:27).

2) Abiding in the Lord—"He who abides in Me [the Lord] and I in him, he bears much fruit" (John 15:5).

The conduct of one who preaches the gospel must be worthy of the Lord's gospel. He also must be one who abides in the Lord and allows the Lord to abide in him, living together with the Lord without any barriers between him and the Lord.

VII. THE AUTHORITY FOR PREACHING
THE GOSPEL

1) The authority of the resurrected Christ—"All authority has been given to Me in heaven and on earth. Go therefore and disciple all the nations" (Matt. 28:18-19). The authority for gospel preaching is all the authority of Christ in heaven and on earth, which transcends all, rules over all, and controls all.

VIII. THE POWER FOR PREACHING
THE GOSPEL

1) The power of the consummate Holy Spirit— "But you shall receive power when the Holy Spirit has come upon you, and you shall be My witnesses... unto the remotest part of the earth" (Acts 1:8). The power for gospel preaching is the very Spirit of power, who is the consummate expression of the Triune God, including the Triune God and all the processes which He has passed through.

IX. HOW TO PREACH THE GOSPEL

1) Praying—"And as they were beseeching...and spoke the word of God with boldness" (Acts 4:31). For the gospel preaching to be effective, one must be a praying person.

2) Being filled outwardly with the Holy Spirit— "They were all filled with the Holy Spirit, and spoke the word of God with boldness" (Acts 4:31). To fulfill our prayer for the preaching of the gospel, there needs to be the outward filling with the Holy Spirit.

3) Following the Spirit—"And the Spirit said to Philip, Approach and join this chariot. And when he ran up..." (Acts 8:29-30). To be able to preach the gospel, express the Lord's life, and bear the fruit of life, one must follow the leading of the Holy Spirit.

4) Being ready in season and out of season— "Preach the word; be ready in season and out of season" (2 Tim. 4:2). In order to preach the gospel with results, one cannot be limited by time.

5) Loving people, spending and being spent for them—"But I will most gladly spend and be utterly spent on behalf of your souls, even if loving you more abundantly, I am loved less" (2 Cor. 12:15). Loving others, spending and being spent for them, is also a wonderful and excellent way to preach the gospel.

6) Speaking the word of God—"...spoke the word of God with boldness" (Acts 4:31). Speaking God's word and not our own is a great secret to successful gospel preaching. To this end, the booklet "The Mystery of Human Life" published by Living Stream Ministry is highly recommended.

7) Visiting from house to house to find the sons of peace—"The harvest indeed is vast, but the workers are few; therefore, beseech the Lord of the harvest that He would thrust out workers into His harvest.

Go on your way... And into whatever house you
enter, first say, Peace to this house. And if a son of
peace is there, your peace shall rest upon it" (Luke
10:2-6). In order that the gospel may be preached in a
widespread manner with plentiful results, the most excellent way is to visit from house to house by knocking on
doors to find the sons of peace and to bring them to believe,
to be baptized, and to be saved.

X. THE REWARD FOR PREACHING
THE GOSPEL

1) Being rewarded—"...preach the gospel. For if
I do this voluntarily, I have a reward" (1 Cor. 9:16-17).
The reward here surely includes the crown of righteousness
mentioned by the Apostle Paul (who also wrote these
words) in 2 Timothy 4:7-8. It is difficult to ascertain what
else this reward will include. In any case, it will surely be
glorious.

XI. THE LOSS OF NOT PREACHING
THE GOSPEL

1) Being woeful—"Woe to me if I do not preach
the gospel" (1 Cor. 9:16). This is a word spoken by the
Apostle Paul, who was faithful through his whole life to
preach the gospel for the Lord. He said that woe would be
to him if he did not preach the gospel. We do not know
what woe may come, but surely it will not be a comfortable
or honorable thing. This should serve as a warning to us!

2) Being taken away—"Every branch in Me [the
Lord] that does not bear fruit, He [the Father] takes
it away" (John 15:2). These are the Lord Jesus' personal
words of warning to us, saying that the Father will take
away every one of His branches which does not bear fruit;
thus, this one will lose all the supply and blessing of being
His branch and of abiding in Him. What a warning this is!

PREACHING OF THE GOSPEL —
RESCUING THE PERISHING

(Hymns, #1358)

Rise! Preach the gos-pel now! Res-cue the fall-en! Lo, mil-lions per-ish-ing dai-ly in pain! Quench not your heart of love, Count not pos-ses-sions: Rise! Preach the gos-pel while mo-ments re-main! Rise! Preach the gos-pel now! Res-cue the fall-en! Your heart of love for them, can you re-strain?

PREACHING OF THE GOSPEL — SOWING

(*Hymns*, #1349)

1 Sowing in the morning, sowing seeds of kindness, Sowing in the noontide and the dewy eve;

Waiting for the harvest, and the time of reaping, We shall come rejoicing, bringing in the sheaves.

CHORUS

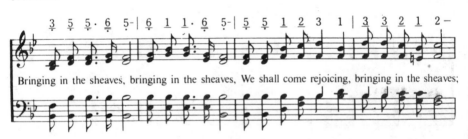

Bringing in the sheaves, bringing in the sheaves, We shall come rejoicing, bringing in the sheaves;

Bringing in the sheaves, bringing in the sheaves, We shall come rejoicing, bringing in the sheaves.

2 Sowing in the sunshine, sowing in the shadows,
Fearing neither clouds nor winter's chilling breeze;
By and by the harvest and the labor ended,
We shall come rejoicing, bringing in the sheaves.

3 Going forth with weeping, sowing for the Master,
Tho' the loss sustained our spirit often grieves;
When our weeping's over, He will bid us welcome,
We shall come rejoicing, bringing in the sheaves.

SERVING THE LORD

Serving the Lord and preaching the gospel are related. After a person is saved, he must preach the gospel and he must serve the Lord. The more a Christian receives grace and is led by the Lord, the more he is delighted to serve the Lord.

I. THE MOTIVE OF SERVING THE LORD

1) "I love my master...I will not go out free" (Exo. 21:5).

A saved person wishes to serve the Lord, not out of others' encouragement or compelling, but out of an inward motive. This motive is his love for the Lord. His love for the Lord constrains him and impels him to serve the Lord. The verse here describes a slave in the Old Testament who, due to his love for his master, would not go out free at the end of his days of slavery; he would rather be a slave to serve his beloved master. This typifies the New Testament believer who should love the Lord and serve Him in the same manner.

2) "I beg you therefore... through the compassions of God to present your bodies a living sacrifice... which is your most reasonable service" (Rom. 12:1).

Here the Apostle Paul begs us to present our bodies as a living sacrifice to serve God. His begging us is through the compassions of God, proving that God's compassions, which are out of God's love, should be our motive in serving God, stirring us up to love God and to serve Him.

II. THE SIGNIFICANCE OF SERVING THE LORD

1) Being a slave of the Lord—"He who was called when free is Christ's slave" (1 Cor. 7:22). To serve the Lord is to be a slave of the Lord Christ. In this verse, a

slave refers to one who is sold and who has lost his freedom. Such a status reveals the significance of serving the Lord. Our serving the Lord is not to do any great work, but to be a slave of Christ to serve the Lord. Thus, in Romans 12:11, the verb used to describe one who serves the Lord is simply the verb form of the word slave and should be translated "serving as a slave."

2) Being priests of God—**"And as they were ministering to the Lord and fasting..."** (Acts 13:2). In the original language, ministering here refers to service as a priest; it is the same word as in Hebrews 10:11 for the "ministering" (serving) of a priest. To serve God as a priest is to handle before God all things related to the worship of God. This requires us to constantly draw near to God and stand before Him.

3) Being the members of Christ's Body—**"But now God has placed the members, each one of them, in the body [of Christ], even as He willed"** (1 Cor. 12:18). We believers are all members placed by God in the Body of Christ, and each member has its function. When we fulfill our office to minister in the Body of Christ according to our function, we are also serving the Lord.

4) Preaching the gospel—**"God... whom I serve... in the gospel of His Son"** (Rom. 1:9). To preach the gospel is also to serve God. This means that we bring sinners to God just as the priests brought sacrifices to offer to God. Thus, Romans 15:16 says that to preach the gospel in this way is to minister "as a priest the gospel of God." This kind of service is valuable, and it fulfills God's eternal economy.

5) Caring for the saints—**"Console the fainthearted, uphold the weak"** (1 Thes. 5:14); **"Communicating to the needs of the saints, pursuing hospitality"** (Rom. 12:13). These words show us that we ought to care for those saints who are immature, weak, sick, needy, or in hardship. This is also a service to the Lord.

6) Serving the church:

1. As an elder—"The elders among you...shepherd the flock of God among you, overseeing... according to God" (1 Pet. 5:1-2). To shepherd and oversee the flock of God, which are the saints in the church, is to serve the church and is quite valuable. This is also a service to the Lord.

2. As a deacon—The word deacon is the noun form of the verb minister. Therefore, a deacon is a serving one who takes care of affairs in the church and ministers to the saints. Such service is of a general nature and is also a service to the Lord.

3. Doing general things—Besides the duties of an elder and those of a deacon, there are many other miscellaneous tasks in the church, such as transporting guests, cleaning and arranging the meeting places, ushering, purchasing, doing clerical work, doing accounting, and serving in the business office, all of which require people's service. These are another category of service to the Lord.

III. HOW TO SERVE THE LORD

1) Serving with our whole being—"Present your bodies"; "be transformed by the renewing of the mind"; "burning in spirit, serving the Lord as a slave" (Rom. 12:1, 2, 11). Our entire being is of three parts: spirit, soul, and body. To serve the Lord with our whole being means that the spirit, soul, and body all participate in the service to the Lord. First, we must present our bodies to the Lord; second, the mind, the main part of our soul, must be renewed and transformed; third, our spirit must be burning. Thus, all three parts of our being participate in serving the Lord.

2) Following the Lord—"If anyone serves Me [the Lord Jesus], let him follow Me; and where I am, there also shall My servant be" (John 12:26). In order to serve the Lord, we must follow the Lord. Those who serve the Lord must take the way which He took. We need to follow the Lord wherever He moves. Where He is, there we also must be. He chose the cross and was willing to take the way of the cross, dying to Himself and to everything. We who follow the Lord must do the same. Thus we will be able to serve Him.

3) According to the counsel of God—"For David indeed, when he had served his own generation by the counsel of God..." (Acts 13:36). Our service to the Lord, like David's, must be according to the counsel of God and in God's counsel.

4) Needing to have an ear to hear—"And his master shall bore his ear through...and he shall serve him for ever" (Exo. 21:6). This says that, in the Old Testament, a master would bore the ear of one who desired to serve, signifying a dealing with his ears that he might be obedient and submissive. To serve the Lord today, we also need the Lord's dealing that we may have the ears to hear and be persons who are obedient and submissive to the Lord.

5) Coming near to and standing before the Lord—"They [the priests] shall come near to me to minister unto me, and they shall stand before me..." (Ezek. 44:15). This verse says that the priests of the Old Testament served God by coming near to God and standing before Him. In order to serve the Lord today, we should do the same. With an ear that can hear the Lord's word, we still must draw near to Him and stand before Him that we may know what the Lord wants us to do so that we can serve Him according to His desire.

6) Being faithful and prudent—"Who then is the faithful and prudent slave, whom the master has set over his household" (Matt. 24:45). As the Lord's slaves who serve Him, we also need to be faithful and prudent. To be faithful is to not be slothful or loose, while to be prudent is to seize the opportunity to accurately complete all the things with which the Lord has commissioned us according

to His will. This is a prerequisite for us who desire to serve the Lord, to be well-pleasing to Him, and to be rewarded at His coming back.

7) Having the loins girded, and the lamps burning, and waiting for the Lord's coming—"Let your loins be girded and your lamps burning... looking for their own lord... when he comes..." (Luke 12:35-36). Here the Lord tells us that to serve Him as His slaves, we need to have our loins girded and our lamps burning, and we need to wait for His return. To have our loins girded means to not be loose, to have the lamps burning is to live in the light, and to wait for the Lord's return is to be watchful. All these are essential qualifications for us who serve the Lord.

8) Coordinating in the Body—"For also the body [of Christ] is not one member but many... If the whole body were an eye, where were the hearing? If the whole were hearing, where were the smelling? But now God has placed the members, each one of them, in the body, even as He willed... But now the members are many, but one body. And the eye cannot say to the hand, I have no need of you; or again the head to the feet, I have no need of you" (1 Cor. 12:14-21). Here we are shown that to serve the Lord as members of the Body of Christ, we must coordinate with the saints and not act independently in the Body of Christ, which is the church. This is also a qualification regarding how we should serve the Lord.

IV. THE GOAL OF SERVING THE LORD

1) Building up the Body of Christ—"Out from whom all the Body, fitted and knit together through every joint of the supply, according to the operation in measure of each one part, causes the growth of the Body unto the building up of itself in love" (Eph. 4:16). This word shows us that our coordination and service with the saints is to cause the growth of the Body of Christ and to build it up in love. Besides saving sinners,

perfecting the saints, and glorifying God (1 Cor. 10:31), our
serving the Lord as His slaves is, even the more, to cause
the Body of Christ to grow and be built up.

V. THE REWARD FOR SERVING THE LORD

**1) Being honored by God the Father—"If anyone
serves Me [the Lord Jesus]... the Father [God] will
honor him"** (John 12:26).

For our service to the Lord, we shall be honored by the
Father. What a reward this is!

**2) Being blessed to sit at the feast and enjoying
the Lord's serving—"Blessed are those slaves whom
the lord when he comes shall find watching... he
will gird himself and will have them recline at the
table, and he will come and serve them"** (Luke 12:37).
This verse says that when the Lord comes back, the slaves
who have been watchful to serve the Lord will be blessed to
sit at the feast and will enjoy the Lord's serving. This is
also a great reward from the Lord to those who serve Him.

**3) Ruling with the Lord and enjoying the joy of
the Lord—"Well done, good and faithful slave... I
will set you over many things; enter into the joy of
your Lord"** (Matt. 25:21, 23). This verse says that the
good and faithful slave who serves the Lord will be set over
many things and enter into the manifestation of the
coming kingdom and into the joy of the Lord. Surely this is
a great reward, which we should appreciate and long for.

VI. THE PUNISHMENT FOR NOT
SERVING THE LORD

**1) Receiving many lashes—"And that slave who
knew his lord's will, and did not prepare or do
according to his will, will receive many lashes"**
(Luke 12:47). The Lord's word here clearly and seriously
tells us that if we who are the Lord's slaves do not serve
Him according to His will, when He comes we will receive
many lashes. To receive lashes is to be punished. The Lord
did not tell us how the punishment will be carried out, but

any punishment, especially that which is repeated many times, is dreadful. May we who have received grace to be the Lord's slaves to serve Him be admonished and warned because of His word.

SERVICE — MINISTERING CHRIST

8.7.8.7.D. (*Hymns*, #912)

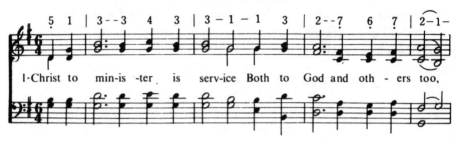

1·Christ to min-is-ter is serv-ice Both to God and oth - ers too,

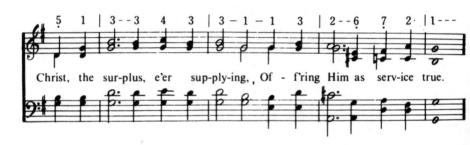

Christ, the sur-plus, e'er sup-ply-ing,, Of - f'ring Him as serv-ice true.

CHORUS

Christ to min-is-ter ' is serv-ice , Both to God and oth-ers too,

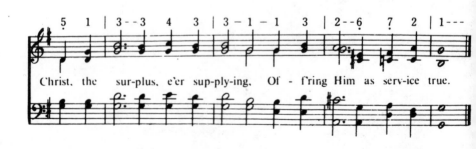

Christ, the sur-plus, e'er sup-ply-ing, Of - f'ring Him as serv-ice true.

2 As the Israelites did offer
From the surplus of their land,
Thus some produce reaped of Jesus
'Must be in our serving hand.

3 We on Christ, as land, must labor,
Harvest Him for all our fare;
Tasting Him to overflowing,
Christ with others we may share.

4 Holding Christ, as members growing,
Each his function must observe;
Christ receiving, Christ partaking,
To His Body Christ we serve.

5 Fellowship and testimony,
Ministry and worship too,
In all helps and ministrations
Christ is all our service true.

THE OFFERING OF MATERIAL RICHES

(It is suggested that this longer lesson be read at two different times, the second beginning from the section on "The Use" on page 103.)

From the time that man developed a problem with God because of the fall and left the position where he took God as everything, material riches have become a critical matter in the life of fallen man. In his fallen condition, man fell into the darkness of acknowledging only material riches and not God, of trusting only in material riches and not in God, and even of serving material riches, taking material riches as God, and allowing material riches to replace God. God's enemy, Satan the Devil, exploited the fallen condition of men to come in and deceive men to worship idols, such as the god of wealth, for riches and gain. By being behind these idols, he supplants men's worship and service that are due God. For this reason, the Lord Jesus told us that one "cannot serve God and mammon" (Matt. 6:24). In the original language, the service mentioned by the Lord here refers to the service of a slave, as we have seen in the previous lesson. This tells us that Satan utilizes material riches to seduce people to worship him on the one hand, and enslaves people in material riches, as misers, on the other hand. However, we have received God's mercy and the Lord's salvation, which delivered us from the authority of Satan and turned us to God (Acts 26:18). After we have received God's salvation in this way, we are confronted with an issue in our practical living, that is, what we should do with material riches that Satan used in time past to delude us and all the world. What should our intention and attitude be toward material riches? How, in particular, should we treat these material riches? Should we be the same as we were in the old manner of living before we were saved? Or should we

have a change regarding our material riches according to
the salvation which delivered us from the authority of
Satan and turned us to God? There are clear instructions
concerning this matter in God's word in the Bible. In the
last twenty-three lessons we covered seventeen subjects
concerning the various crucial matters between us and
God. Now we shall consider the matter of the offering of
material riches.

I. GOD'S GIVING

1) **"Nor to set their hope on the uncertainty of
riches, but on God who affords us all things richly
for our enjoyment"** (1 Tim. 6:17). This word exposes
Satan's plot to delude men, showing us that all the
material things and enjoyment in our living apparently
come from the uncertain riches, but they actually come
from God's giving. They are supplied to us from God's rich
giving. Hence, we must not set our hope on deceitful and
uncertain material riches, but on the very God who gives
us all things for our enjoyment.

2) **"Beloved, concerning all things I wish that you
may prosper"** (3 John 2). The prosperity here refers to
material abundance and prosperity, pointing out that the
material enjoyment of those who are saved and belong to
God comes from God as a result of His prospering our
material things. We ought to endeavor in our businesses.
The Bible also requires that we learn to maintain good
works for necessary needs (Titus 3:14, 8). Yet without God's
blessing, all our labors, endeavorings, and painstaking
enterprises will yield little. Therefore, in this matter of
material supply, unlike the worldly people who trust only
in their own abilities, we have to learn to set our hope in
God.

3) **"Now He who bountifully supplies seed to the
sower..."** (2 Cor. 9:10). The Bible regards the offering of
material riches as sowing. The seed is supplied by God and
comes from God. This reveals that the material riches
which the believers offer to God come originally from God

and are given by God. We are thus offering to God what He has given to us.

II. THE LORD'S CHARGE

1) "Do not lay up for yourselves treasures on the earth... but lay up for yourselves treasures in heaven" (Matt. 6:19-20). We need to look at this word of the Lord from the viewpoint of laying up material riches. To lay up material riches is to save what is left of a man's gain after the needs of his living have been met. Here, the Lord charges us not to lay up these surplus riches on the earth, but to lay them up in heaven, that is, to spend them on the heavenly Father, doing such things as helping those in need, thus making friends with them (Luke 16:9) and advancing His gospel (Phil. 1:5).

2) "Charge those who are rich in the present age not to be high-minded, nor to set their hope on the uncertainty of riches, but on God who affords us all things richly for our enjoyment; to do good, to be rich in good works, ready to distribute, willing to communicate, laying away for themselves as a treasure a good foundation for the future, that they may lay hold on that which is really life" (1 Tim. 6:17-19). This is the apostle's charge, which is simply the Lord's charge to us. The rich refers to those who have excess from their gain after the needs of their living have been met. To do good and to be rich in good works refer to distributing the surplus from one's living to the needy ones. To be rich in doing good and good works is to be ready to distribute and willing to communicate. This is also to lay up treasure in heaven, to lay up as a treasure a good foundation for the future. Doing this will enable one to lay hold on, that is, to possess, to use, and to enjoy, that which is really life, the eternal life of God. To save up the surplus riches from our living on the earth is to lay hold on and make use of our natural life; while to save up the same in heaven, spending it on God, is to lay hold on and employ the eternal life of God.

III. THE LORD'S PROMISE

1) "Give, and it will be given to you; good measure, pressed down, shaken together, running over, they will give into your bosom" (Luke 6:38). This is a promise spoken from the Lord's own mouth. If we are willing to distribute our material wealth to the needy for God's sake, He will surely give into our bosom that which is rich and plenteous, a good measure, pressed down, shaken together, running over. He will not give into our hands that which is scanty and limited. What a profitable deal this is!

2) "Remember the words of the Lord Jesus which He Himself said, It is more blessed to give than to receive" (Acts 20:35). Concerning material riches, human beings, who are deceived by Satan, will only receive and not give. To want to receive and not give is Satan's ploy, which causes man to lose God's blessing. The best way to be blessed by God in material riches is to give, not to receive, just as the Lord Himself did for us. Thus, the Lord Himself promised us that it is more blessed to give than to receive. Myriads of believers throughout the ages who have believed in the Lord's word and who have practiced accordingly confirm the trustworthiness of this promise from their experience.

3) "He who sows sparingly, sparingly also shall reap; and he who sows with blessings, with blessings also shall reap" (2 Cor. 9:6). This is a natural law established by the Lord in the biological realm. This law contains His promise. Offering material riches is like sowing. Since sowing eventually brings in reaping, he who sows sparingly shall reap sparingly, and he who sows bountifully shall reap bountifully. In man's eyes, the offering of material riches is to give away their riches. However, in God's eyes, such offering is a kind of sowing which will result in reaping. He who offers little shall reap little, and he who offers much shall reap much. We ought to believe in the Lord's promise in this law.

4) "Bring ye all the tithes into the storehouse, that there may be meat in mine house, and prove me now herewith, saith the Lord of hosts, if I will not open you the windows of heaven, and pour you out a blessing, that there shall not be room enough to receive it" (Mal. 3:10). The "tithes" are the legal amount of offering which God required from the harvest of the Israelites in the Old Testament. The "storehouse" refers to the place in the Old Testament temple where all the offerings to God from His people were stored. My "house" refers to God's temple in the Old Testament. This word superabundantly displays the infinitely rich promise of God. Although it was spoken to the Israelites in the Old Testament, in principle it applies also to the New Testament believers. If we will fully offer to God what belongs to Him that the church may be richly supplied, God will open the windows of heaven for us and pour out a blessing to us, which there will not be enough room to contain. This is a solemn promise of the Lord of hosts. We can offer to Him according to His promise to prove Him.

IV. THE USE

1) **For the need of the church—** In the Old Testament, God wanted each of His people, the Israelites, to offer to Him a ransom for his soul. This offering was for the use of God's dwelling place, that is, the tabernacle and the temple (Exo. 30:11-16). The church today is God's real tabernacle (dwelling place—Eph. 2:22) and real temple (1 Cor. 3:16-17). We, all the New Testament believers, also should offer to God to meet the needs of the different expenses in the church where we are.

2) **For the advancement of the gospel—**"For your fellowship unto the gospel from the first day until now" (Phil. 1:5). Fellowship in this verse refers to participation and enjoyment. From the first day when they were saved to the time when Paul wrote this epistle to them, the Philippian believers continuously supplied the needs of Paul with material riches in his gospel preaching

for the advancement of the gospel. Thus they participated and enjoyed with Paul in the advancement of the gospel. This tells us that once we are saved, we should offer to God the rich surplus from our material riches, which He gives us for the advancement of His gospel.

3) **Supplying the Lord's servants—"Philippians...** **you sent both once and again to my [the Apostle** **Paul's] need"** (Phil. 4:15-16). Those who serve the Lord with their full time have no time to make a living by a profession. Thus, there is a need for the believers to supply them with the material riches they offer to the Lord. First Timothy 5:17 tells us that the believers ought to supply material riches to the elders who take the lead well and those who labor in God's word and teaching (the local elders).

4) **Supplying the needy saints:**

1. **"Communicating to the needs of the saints"** (Rom. 12:13). This verse shows that we should supply the lacking or needy saints with material riches. This is also one of the uses of our offering of material riches.

2. **"Only that we should remember the poor"** (Gal. 2:10). We should also remember the poor (with the stress on the poor among the believers), supplying them with the material riches we have received from God.

V. THE AMOUNT

1) **"...according as any one of them was pros-** **pered, determined each one of them to send things** **for dispensing"** (Acts 11:29); **"Let each one of you lay** **aside by himself, storing up as he may be pros-** **pered..."** (1 Cor. 16:2). We have seen previously that, according to 3 John 2, prosperity is God's blessing to prosper us. We should determine the amount of our offering to God based upon the condition of our being prospered due to His blessing. Each person should determine his own amount according to whatever he has, not according to what he does not have (2 Cor. 8:12).

2) "He who sows sparingly, sparingly also shall reap; and he who sows with blessings, with blessings also shall reap; each one as he has purposed in his heart, not out of sorrow or of necessity, for God loves a cheerful giver" (2 Cor. 9:6-7). In our offering of material riches, we will reap little if we sow little, and we will reap much if we sow much. Each person should purpose in his own heart how much he should offer without sorrow or necessity, since God loves him who is a cheerful giver.

VI. THE WAY

1) "With much entreaty beseeching of us the grace and the fellowship of the ministry to the saints; and . . . they gave themselves first to the Lord, and to us through the will of God" (2 Cor. 8:4-5). The churches in Macedonia supplied their material riches to the needy saints in Judea, on the one hand, by beseeching the apostles for a share in the grace and the fellowship of such ministry, and on the other hand, by giving themselves first to the Lord and then to the apostles through the will of God. This shows us that the offering of material riches which is most acceptable to the Lord is the offering of ourselves first to the Lord and then to the apostles, who are concerned for us, eventually asking them for a share in such grace and fellowship.

2) "But take heed not to do your righteousness [giving alms] before men to be gazed at by them; otherwise, you surely have no reward with your Father who is in the heavens. When therefore you give alms, do not sound a trumpet before you as the hypocrites do in the synagogues and in the streets that they may be glorified by men. Truly I say to you, They have their reward. But you, when you give alms, let not your left hand know what your right hand is doing, so that your alms may be in secret; and your Father who sees in secret shall repay you" (Matt. 6:1-4). For whatever use we offer our

material riches, we must not do it intentionally for others to see in order that we may be glorified and rewarded by men; otherwise, we will not be rewarded by the Father, who is in the heavens. Therefore, we should not let our left hand know what our right hand is doing. We should offer in secret that the heavenly Father, who sees what we do, may repay us, recompensing and rewarding us according to His promises to us mentioned earlier.

According to the Lord's charge in these words, we should do our best not to let others know of our offering of material riches. Either named donations or open contributions must be avoided. For this reason, we have set up offering boxes in the meeting places in order to allow the saints to drop their offering into these boxes in a secret way. This matches the way God's people in the Old Testament put their money into the chest (2 Kings 12:9).

VII. THE SIGNIFICANCE

1) Fellowship with the receiver—"the fellowship of the ministry to the saints" (2 Cor. 8:4). Supplying the saints with material riches is a fellowship which brings mutual grace to both the giver and the receiver.

2) Righteousness toward men before God—"He gave to the poor, his righteousness abides forever" (2 Cor. 9:9). Giving material riches to the poor is righteousness toward men before God. God cares for the poor and wants His people also to care for them (Deut. 15:7-8). "He that hath pity upon the poor lendeth unto the Lord" (Prov. 19:17). This is a law established by God which regulates the relationship between human beings. Thus, if we practice according to this law of God, our righteousness toward men before God will abide forever. In the constitution of the kingdom, the Lord Jesus also considered our giving of alms as righteousness (Matt. 6:1-4). If we who live in the Lord's kingdom of the heavens do not give alms and do not give our material riches for God's use, we are breaking the highest law of the kingdom. Giving to the poor the material riches that God has given to us is not only goodness (Heb. 13:16) but also righteousness. We may or may not do good, but it is imperative that we do righteousness since it is our duty. If we fail to do righteousness, we are unrighteous toward men before God.

3) A sacrifice well-pleasing to God—"But do not be forgetful doing good and sharing with others, for with such sacrifices God is well pleased" (Heb. 13:16); "Receiving...the things from you, a fragrant odor, an acceptable sacrifice, well-pleasing to God" (Phil. 4:18). Here doing good refers to the distribution of material riches to others, which before God is a well-pleasing sacrifice to God. Our offering of material things to God's servants is also an acceptable sacrifice which is well-pleasing to God.

4) A fragrant odor well-pleasing to God—"Receiving...the things from you, a fragrant odor, an acceptable sacrifice, well-pleasing to God" (Phil. 4:18). The fragrant odor here refers to the sweet savor of the burnt offering (Gen. 8:20-21; Lev. 1:9). The offering we give to God's servants is not only a sacrifice to God, but also a fragrant odor of a burnt offering that is well-pleasing to God. This reveals that the sacrifice here is like a burnt offering that is satisfying and well-pleasing to God.

The four significances of the offering of material riches mentioned above should show us the importance and value of such offering. By being offered to God for God's use by us who are of God, what was considered by God as "mammon of unrighteousness" (Luke 16:9), that is, as deceitful riches (Matt. 13:22) and uncertain riches (1 Tim. 6:17) which will "fail" (Luke 16:9), can actually become our "fellowship" with the saints, our "righteousness" toward men before God, an acceptable "sacrifice" to God, and a well-pleasing "fragrant odor" to Him. Riches that deceive men, corrupt men, and destroy men can actually become such transcendent blessings that we have before God! This is all a result of our offering of material riches.

CONSECRATION — SURRENDERING ALL TO THE LORD

7.7.7.7. with chorus. (*Hymns*, #1359)

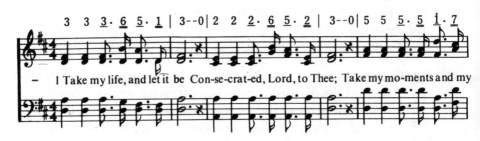

- I Take my life, and let it be Con-se-crat-ed, Lord, to Thee; Take my mo-ments and my

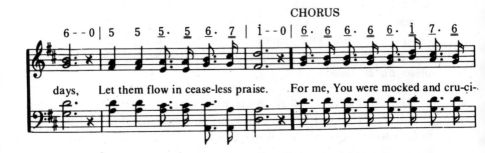

CHORUS

days, Let them flow in cease-less praise. For me, You were mocked and cru-ci-

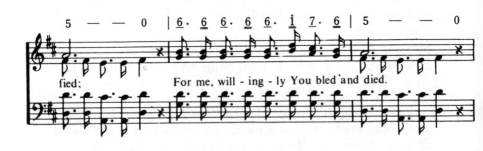

fied; For me, will-ing-ly You bled and died.

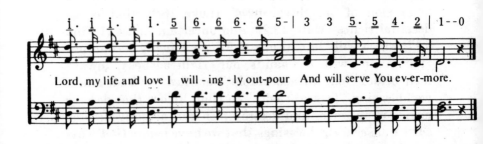

Lord, my life and love I will-ing-ly out-pour And will serve You ev-er-more.

2 Take my hands and feet, I pray
   For Thy work, to run Thy way.
   Take my lips that I may sound
   Words of truth to those around.

3 Take my silver and my gold;
   Not a mite would I withhold.
   Take my intellect, and use
   Every power as Thou shalt choose.

4 Make my heart and will Thine own;
   They belong to Thee alone.
   Take my love; my Lord, I pour
   At Thy feet its treasure-store.

5 Take me, Lord, till I've become
   Ever joined to Thee as one.
   Take myself, and I will be
   Ever, only, all for Thee.